Many are disillusioned with the institutional church today, so some are experimenting with creative forms of church. In the midst of the confusion, Bruce Milne's voice deserves to be heard. Here is a book about the church that rests on the twin authorities of Scripture and experience. He illustrates the biblical vision of the church as a 'new humanity' from his years of experience in ministry in downtown Vancouver. He knows that what the Bible claims works! He never shirks the hard question and regularly provides a practical answer. Whether we are complacent conservatives or radical misfits, here is an invitation worth accepting to rethink church and bring it more into line with God's heart and purpose.

*Dr Derek Tidball, Principal, London School of Theology*

This is an invaluable, scholarly and accessible tool for all leaders and thinking Christians who want to grapple with the challenges and privileges of holding unity in diversity.

*Joel Edwards, General Director, Evangelical Alliance*

D0177146

# DYNAMIC

# DIVERSITY

I wonder if anything is more urgent today, for the honour of Christ and for the spread of the gospel, than that the church should be, and should be seen to be, what by God's purpose and Christ's achievement it already is – a single new humanity, a model of human community; a family of reconciled brothers and sisters who love their Father and who love each other, the evident dwelling place of God by his Spirit. Only then will the world believe in Christ as Peacemaker. Only then will God receive the glory due to his name.

John Stott, *God's New Society*

**Bruce Milne**

# DYNAMIC DIVERSITY

2006.

## The new humanity church for today and tomorrow

INTER-VARSITY PRESS
Norton Street, Nottingham NG7 3HR, England
Email: ivp@ivpbooks.com
Website: www.ivpbooks.com

*First published 2006*

**British Library Cataloguing in Publication Data**
A catalogue record for this book is available from the British Library.

UK ISBN-13: 978–1–84474–158–8
UK ISBN-10: 1–84474–158–3

Set in Dante 10.5/13pt
Typeset in Great Britain by CRB Associates, Reepham, Norfolk
Printed and bound in Great Britain by Creative Print and Design (Wales),
Ebbw Vale

Inter-Varsity Press publishes Christian books that are true to the Bible and that
communicate the gospel, develop discipleship and strengthen the church for its
mission in the world.

Inter-Varsity Press is closely linked with the Universities and Colleges Christian
Fellowship, a student movement connecting Christian Unions in universities
and colleges throughout Great Britain, and a member movement of the
International Fellowship of Evangelical Students. Website: *www.uccf.org.uk*

# Contents

# Preface

We are all familiar with a Mexican wave. A sports event is under way in a large stadium. The action on the field is rather boring, when suddenly the spectators in one section of the audience jump to their feet and throw their arms in the air. The next section follows on, and then the next, until the wave has travelled all around the stadium, and back to the beginning, where it may well set off all over again. It's great fun, and often notably more memorable than what's happening on the field of play.

Every Sunday of the year a 'Mexican wave of worship' travels all around the world. Let me tell you about it.

It begins about the time many in the United Kingdom are heading off for bed on Saturday night (and not a few of its pastors are staggering wearily out of their studies). For many North Americans the wave is launched while we are fast asleep. But, just then, in some South Pacific islands, like the ancient Christian Kingdom of Tonga, it's Sunday morning, and already Christians are up and heading for church, where they are called to worship. They get on their feet, many thousands of them, throwing their hands in the air, as it were, praising God, and crying, 'Jesus is Lord!' The wave has begun.

At the very same time, thousands of miles to the north, in the eastern reaches of the former Soviet empire, other groups of believers are doing the same – fewer in number but with no less zeal.

Then the wave begins to spread westwards; into New Zealand, and across Australia, through time zone after time zone, millions are now on their feet and joining in. Meanwhile, the worship wave is sweeping down eastern Asia; reaching to the smaller churches of Japan, the teeming congregations of South Korea, the Philippines and Indonesia. The living God is being worshipped and his name exalted. Now the wave is into China – how many Christians in China? Only God knows; perhaps a hundred million, province after province, as the wave of worship sweeps on its way around the world.

Now the wave is into India and the great historic churches there, and then surging on through the other southern Asian nations. On and on it moves, across the vast territories of Central Asia and the former Soviet republics, into the Middle East, where little groups of believers are uniting in worship and bravely lifting heart and hand in praise. Now the wave has entered Africa; the ancient churches of Egypt and Ethiopia, and the massive, modern congregations of Uganda, Kenya and Zambia; on down into Southern Africa as millions more are on their feet and the Lord is being exalted. Now the wave is across central Africa and sweeping through the burgeoning congregations in Nigeria, Ghana and the adjoining nations. And all the while Europe has been caught up in it, through time zone after time zone – the Scandinavian lands to the north, the Balkans, Central Europe and the Mediterranean countries to the south, all with their long centuries of faith and tradition; then it's into Spain and Portugal.

Meanwhile, the worship wave is moving through Britain, by way of congregations large and small, in city and countryside, as UK Christians in turn rise to their feet and join the global throng of worshippers, lifting high the name of Jesus. Now the wave is leaping across the sea to Ireland, Iceland and Greenland, finally arriving on North American soil in the maritime provinces of Canada; and, at the same moment, thousands of kilometres to the south, it is making its landfall in Latin America by way of the bulging projection of Brazil, where it is soon swelled by that nation's thronging multitudes of exuberant worshippers.

Like an irresistible tide the wave sweeps on, gathering millions more in its train as our ever-blessed, triune God is exalted in praise. On and on it goes, as the sunny islands of the Caribbean get with the beat, down the east coast of the USA amid its teeming populations. Meanwhile, to the south, the wave envelops in turn all the nations of central and western Latin America, Argentina, Chile, Peru, Bolivia,

Mexico and the swelling churches of Central America. Across the Canadian prairies it moves, and the Midwest of the USA, and through the Deep South. Finally it arrives at the western states, California, Oregon, Washington, and, within that time zone, at our apparently 'lazy lot' in Vancouver, as we too get out of our beds, and assemble in worship, and lift Jesus' name, and pour out our praises.

And then the wave of worship is on its way again, up to Alaska, and across the Pacific to Hawaii, and, in a final surge, back to the South Sea Islands – and it is over for another week: the worship wave!

It happens without fail every single Sunday, of every month of every year, and all I have done in these paragraphs is to draw attention to it – the international celebration of the global people of God.[1] To be a Christian means to be part of *that* – somewhere between one and two billion men, women and children, from every nation under the sun, united in a worship experience that encircles the globe. How could anyone miss out on it by choosing to stay in bed?

This global Sunday community is of course staggeringly diverse. What contrasts of race and ethnicity are here! What ranges of generation and gender, language and culture, customs and worship styles, social status and wealth indices, educational levels and forms of employment; what degrees of freedom, involving in some places intrusive restrictions and even persecution; what varieties of personal faith stories, and levels of comprehension and commitment! Yet all of that incredible diversity has a single, authentic point of unity: Jesus Christ. In the supernatural reality of his risen presence through the Holy Spirit, that multi-faceted community is *one* as his body on earth. In Jesus they are *one* people, *one* life.

This book is written in the conviction that that divine mystery, the diversity in unity of the people of God in Christ, need not be confined to the global stage, nor need it be deferred to the future age of glory (Dan. 7:14; Rev. 7:9). Rather, it can be experienced today, in embryo, in every local Christian congregation on the face of the earth, as major forms of human diversity are transcended in the supernatural unity of the body of Christ. And, further, to set about, under God, consciously to create such localized expressions of diversity in unity is a major means of bringing glory to the Lord Jesus Christ in our generation, as well as being a supreme missional attraction in our twenty-first-century cultures.

Nor is that an extravagant claim, because *it has in fact happened before* – in the fledgling congregations that burst into life across the Roman Empire in the decades immediately following the ministry, death and rising of Jesus Christ. While never perfect, as the New Testament bears witness, these congregations nevertheless discovered a radically new quality of communal life in which natural diversities of ethnicity, race[2] and every other major human diversity were overcome in a way that astonished, fascinated and finally won a multitude of followers from the watching world around them.

It is my conviction that this feature of first-century history is recoverable today; that there is a way of 'doing church' in these early years of the third millennium that can capture the vibrancy of global community and unite Christians locally across the threatening polarities that bedevil our world. In the process it offers a form of Christian faith that is both deeply relevant and hugely attractive.

I refer to such congregations as 'new-humanity' churches (Eph. 2:15), for reasons that will become apparent in the chapters that follow.

Congregations come, of course, in different shapes and sizes, for, in our highly diverse society, rather as in the variegated communities we meet in the pages of the New Testament, one size can never fit all. But there is a series of common characteristics, arising out of a quite specific vision of what local churches are intended by God to be, which permits a common label, and which accordingly makes this book possible. I invite you to accompany me as I attempt to justify that claim in the following pages.

Lest all this appear dangerously theoretical, may I note that the chapters that follow emerge out of first-hand experience. In the goodness of God, during a seventeen-year ministry at the heart of North America's most secularized community, I had the privilege, along with a special congregation, of glimpsing that vision and fleshing out some of its more basic features, as many hundreds of lost and lonely people found the deepest longings of their hearts met in Jesus Christ and his church. For, incredible as it may sound to a generation where 'church' is commonly our greatest evangelistic liability, during these years in Vancouver, the congregation was actually our best evangelist.

Not that this little volume is yet another 'Do it my way' church blueprint. Transferability between congregations is, in my judgment, a vastly overrated commodity. Hence, the occasions on which our

Vancouver experience is cited in the following pages will be relatively few. What is much more important than one local church's experience is the fact, as I will seek to demonstrate below, that the principles underlying a new-humanity congregation are actually underwritten in the Scriptures, as well as by the great historic doctrines of the faith. On that universally relevant basis the case will be argued.

In the later chapters I will attempt to bring the new-humanity model down to earth by noting its contribution in the areas of worship, leadership, discipleship, fellowship and evangelism.

The book is written primarily for pastors and other church leaders who face the challenge of providing input to the vision and direction of their congregations. However, many of the issues discussed will resonate with, and hopefully be helpful to, any concerned and thinking church member.

An early version of the theme was presented as the Dr George Beasley-Murray Memorial Lecture in Birmingham, England, during the Baptist World Alliance Congress in July 2005. I am deeply appreciative of the trustees of that lectureship for the opportunity to contribute to the honour of a great Christian scholar and leader, who was one of my supreme life mentors.

My thanks are due to the many who have stimulated and influenced me over the years, most obviously our congregation in Vancouver. Within that company may I express particular appreciation to my prayer-support group of many years, Phyllis Metcalfe, Bill Patey, Nancy Scambler and Gord Taylor, who, as well as being ever-faithful intercessors, acted as research associates. I have benefited also from the reflections of Paul Pearce and Vic Arneill in the later stages of the production of this manuscript. Eleanor Trotter of IVP was a helpful and caring support during the process of its production. My wife, Valerie, was, as she always has been, a source of unfailing encouragement throughout. To these, and other friends too numerous to name, I dedicate these pages.

*Bruce Milne*
*Vancouver*
*Ascension, 2006*

# 1 What's this 'new-humanity' thing?

The Balkan War of 1992–5 took 250,000 lives. It also claimed the dubious honour of contributing a new phrase to the bloody history of human conflict: 'ethnic cleansing'. In the uneasy peace which has ensued between the now partitioned communities of Bosnians, Croats and Serbs, only one group has been able to bridge the yawning gulfs and bring people together from the three communities – the evangelical Christians.[1]

This achievement would not have surprised the apostle Paul. In his letter to the Ephesians he claims that Christians are a new kind of people, forming a new kind and quality of community – a new humanity in Christ (Eph. 2:15).

Everywhere in today's world diversity meets us. From the footpaths of our cities to the chatrooms of the Internet, people are connecting today as never before, across the great traditional divides of gender, race, ethnicity and generation. Unhappily, however, these contacts are often less than benign. The 'different' stranger is commonly a threat to be resisted rather than a friend to be embraced. Mini-Balkans dot the planet, and threatening confrontations undermine all the utopian dreams of human brotherhood.

As the planet shrinks through the multiple forces of immigration, travel, electronic communication and more fluid employment patterns, we find ourselves forced into contact, to a degree never before experienced on planet Earth, with those who are significantly different from ourselves: the family that has moved in next door, the work colleague at the next computer, the student across the corridor in the halls of residence, the occupant of the neighbouring seat on a plane, the user of the next exercise machine at our gym. Amid the countless human connections which fill out our days, difference and diversity are increasingly prominent.

In today's context of in-your-face diversity, it is time to revisit the heart of the New Testament, with its claim that in Jesus Christ a new quality of human relationships has arrived and that the gatherings of his followers in Christian churches represent a unique possibility of bridging the gulfs that separate. The assertion of this book is that all Christian congregations, everywhere, are called to be just that – bridging-places, centres of reconciliation, where all the major diversities which separate human beings are overcome through the supernatural presence of the Holy Spirit.

We can unpack this claim in nine propositions, which will form the thread of the argument through the following chapters.

1. We are called today to intentionally develop local churches in which the primary human polarities are transcended in a supernatural 'life together' in Jesus Christ.
2. The diversities that are to be transcended include those of gender, generation, ethnicity, race, colour, family unit, social and economic status, educational opportunity, mental and physical health experience, spiritual history, spiritual gifting and personality type.
3. Such 'diversity-in-unity' congregations are a powerful demonstration in today's world of God's age-long purpose to 'bring all things in heaven and on earth together under one head, even Christ' (Eph. 1:10).
4. Such congregations are an expression of the 'new humanity' that is the direct fruit of the reconciling ministry of Jesus Christ on the cross. They are accordingly a witness to, and an honouring of, our Lord Jesus Christ and his sacrifice.

5. Such new-humanity congregations are not a natural, human possibility. They become possible only through the ministry of the Holy Spirit, whose primary gift and fruit is self-denying love.

6. Such new-humanity congregations are underwritten by New Testament teaching (Jesus in the Gospels; the apostles in their letters), and by New Testament experience (the Acts). They are also deeply congruent with major Christian doctrines such as the Trinity, the incarnation and the future hope.

7. New-humanity congregations give expression to the deep-seated longing in the human heart for a life in community which embraces the breadth of the human family. This was a major secret of their manifest attractiveness in the first century.

8. New-humanity congregations carry the potential for a similar powerful attractiveness in today's and tomorrow's worlds, where unprecedented diversity, with its potential for conflict, will increasingly characterize local and global society.

9. New-humanity congregations offer a unique, biblically mandated means of witnessing to God's purpose in history, of fulfilling the Great Commission and the Great Commandments of Jesus, of experiencing rich relational fulfilment, and of being a sign of the presence of God's kingdom as well as anticipating its final triumph, and hence are a supreme means of glorifying the triune God.

## Ephesians: a 'big-picture' letter

Like all good sermons, we begin from a text, '[Christ's] purpose was to create in himself *one new humanity*' (Eph. 2:15). What does Paul mean by that? What are its implications for how we 'do church' today? Answering these questions requires us to set Ephesians 2:15 in a larger biblical context.

Starting in this way with Scripture is not an option but a necessity. What really matters about churches is what God thinks about them, which means listening to what he says in the inspired words of the Bible. Only what accords with that has any final validity or universal relevance. Our experience of church does have to be weighed, and we also need to be alert to the winds of change in our culture; we will attempt to do both of these in the chapters below. But neither of these factors can set our agenda or give our conclusions final validity.

Accordingly, the first part of this book will examine the biblical evidence that supports the propositions above. This will take some time, but unless we do so the more practical sections which follow are devoid of general significance. In the area of church, more than any other, simply inviting others to 'do things the way *we* did it' has led too many congregations into fruitless bypaths. So, 'Speak Lord . . . ' – which brings us back to Ephesians.

In 1997 I stood on the site of the Herodian prison in Caesarea, on the north-west coast of Palestine. As I gazed out into the great, tumbling Mediterranean breakers crashing onto the beach, I thought of Paul. This was the very spot where he was imprisoned for two years awaiting trial (Acts 24:27). It was impossible to forget, too, that at the further reaches of that very sea lay the ruins of ancient Rome, from so many points of view the centre of Paul's inherited world, the 'Eternal City' to which the apostle would be taken from Caesarea, for further incarceration prior to his arraignment before Caesar.

It was during the enforced leisure of these imprisonments that, in all likelihood, Paul wrote Ephesians, and that evocative geographical setting in Caesarea may arguably have influenced his theme. For Ephesians is a 'big-picture' writing, which ranges far and wide across the vistas of God's age-long redemptive plan, to answer our 'big-picture' questions, not least concerning the place of the church in the purpose of God.

### The plan of the ages

To come to closer quarters, the theme of this carefully crafted writing lies at 1:10, where Paul states the goal of God's entire salvation process: 'his good pleasure, which he purposed in Christ, to bring all things in heaven and earth together under one head, even Christ'.[2]

Thus the culmination of all God's purposes, the destiny towards which all that he has made and sustains in the physical and spiritual creation is moving, is here announced: 'to bring all things . . . together under Christ' – to crown all things with Christ. What a magnificent, thrilling perspective! There is something within every Christian heart that is ready to leap to its feet and cry out to a listening church and world: 'Behold, the Lamb upon the throne. Crown him with many crowns! To him be the glory for ever and ever!'

The phrase 'all things together under' translates a single Greek word with a vivid usage in Greek mathematics. When the Greeks wished to add a series of numbers together, they habitually listed these, rather as we still do (assuming no calculator is to hand), by writing them one under the other in a column. However, whereas we today tend to draw a line at the *foot* of the list, and write the total *beneath* the line, the Greeks tended to draw the line *above* the column and put the total *above* the line. Hence they (literally) 'summed *up*'. Paul here sees God drawing a line across the entire human and superhuman story, and writing 'Jesus Christ' 'above the line' as his 'summing up' of all things.

Nor is this anticipation merely a matter of wishful thinking, for the enthronement of Christ has already been achieved. It was realized in his resurrection, by which God 'raised him from the dead and seated him at his right hand in the heavenly realms, far above all rule and authority, power and dominion, and every title that can be given, not only in the present age but also in the one to come' (Eph. 1:20–21). Nothing less was the claim of the risen Jesus himself: 'All authority in heaven and on earth has been given to me' (Matt. 28:18).

The Christian centuries have not lacked testimony to its truth. One thinks of Luther, as the German princes, fearful for his safety, tried to dissuade him from his perilous journey to Augsburg: 'At Augsburg are the powers of hell!' But the reformer would have none of their craven capitulation. 'And at Augsburg', he shouted, 'Jesus reigns!'

The conviction that this is so, that in his Easter passage from death to life Jesus has moved to a place of unqualifiable sovereignty over all things, and hence that there is now, in this post-Easter world, a crucified carpenter from Nazareth on the throne of this universe – *that* was the daring, defiant conviction which galvanized the first Christian community, and which finds untiring emphasis within the pages of the New Testament. It was, as Denney noted, 'the first, and last and dominating element in the Christian consciousness of the New Testament'.[3]

### Your King is coming!

The Christian anticipation of the future, as expressed in Ephesians 1:10, is that that reign, already entered upon, will be fully realized for, and acknowledged by, all conceivable orders of existence. This does not imply that all will acknowledge Christ's reign in glad submission (cf. 5:6, 'God's wrath comes on those who are disobedient'). Nonetheless, whether with ecstatic joy (in the case of the redeemed) or in trembling dread (for those beings, both human and superhuman, who continue in rebellious impenitence), *all* in earth and heaven, whether in joy or in judgment, *will* acknowledge this King. The final goal is therefore profoundly Christ-centred and comprehensive. The Lord Jesus Christ, he and no other, will wear the crown on that day. We resonate to Paul Kauffman's great sentence: 'Tomorrow's history has already been written . . . at the name of Jesus every knee will bow!'

We should note also that since this is the *divine* purpose, it is not merely a possibility to be aimed for, but a destiny to be infallibly realized. Since this is the purpose of the God 'who works out everything in conformity with the purpose of his will (1:11), in a real sense it is already accomplished. 'All things together under Christ' – that is the future. Quite simply it is *your* tomorrow, and mine. It is inscribed on every calendar in heaven, and, however unacknowledged, it is also etched into every calendar on earth. To this, every life – your life, my life, all life – is moving, whether terrestrial or celestial, and every passing second is a step closer to its realization.

*It's already here!*
Having stated the glorious divine purpose in the opening sentences of Ephesians, Paul proceeds to explore it in the following paragraphs. And a wonderfully encouraging conviction energizes his development of the theme – one that is crucial to the argument of this book: *this glorious purpose is not wholly future*. Paul is convinced that it has already erupted into space-time history.

The historic 'firstfruits' of God's triumphant purpose operate at two discernible points, corresponding, not surprisingly, to the two dimensions of the purpose referred to at 1:10: 'under . . . Christ', the headship feature, and 'together', the unification feature – *both*, Paul proceeds to claim, are already in evidence.

As far as the 'headship' is concerned, Paul points, as we noted a moment ago, to the historic resurrection of Jesus, by which God established him 'at his right hand in the heavenly realms, far above all rule and authority, power and dominion' (1:20–21). The unification ('together') aspect comes to the centre from 2:11 onwards, a purpose now evident *in the church*, expressed in embryonic form in the relationship of Christian Jews with Christian Gentiles. Accordingly, in keeping with the thrust of both the letter and this book, we pause to contemplate the unity of Jew and Gentile in the church, and with it the firstfruits of the new humanity.

## Ephesians 2:11–18

### No-man's-land

Prior to Christ's coming, the prospects for community between Jew and Gentile were bleak in the extreme. In Hendriksen's succinct paraphrase of 2:12, the Gentiles 'BC' were 'Christless, friendless, stateless, hopeless and Godless'.[4]

Not surprisingly, this religious divide was accompanied by a deep attitudinal antipathy. Paul calls it, without exaggeration, 'hostility' (2:14, 16). Secular and Christian writers combine to emphasize the depth of this mutual hatred. Tacitus (c. 55–120), for example, claimed that the Jews 'regard the rest of mankind with all the hatred of enemies'.[5] Barclay summarizes the relationship: 'The Jew had an immense contempt for the Gentile. The Gentiles, said the Jews, were created by God to be fuel for the fires of hell. God, they said, loves only Israel of all the nations that he has made.'[6]

This religious divide, with its fermenting hostility, fixed a great gulf between Jew and Gentile. Into that spiritual no-man's-land had come, in the fullness of time, Jesus the Christ. With his life, ministry, self-sacrifice and resurrection, the entire landscape had been altered. Paul signals that with a great adversative, 'But now . . .' (2:13), as he moves on to celebrate the wonder of God's reconciliation of Jew and Gentile in Jesus. For by him the Gentiles, who, as we saw above (2:12), were profoundly estranged from God and his salvation, have now been 'brought near'. The intractable enemies have been reconciled and become friends.

### One at the cross

The specific means is not the ministry of Jesus in general, but its central act of atonement in particular; the Gentiles are 'brought near through the blood of Christ' (2:13). Following his master, Paul affirms that the new, inclusive covenant between God and humanity is established 'in [Christ's] blood' (1 Cor. 11:25). The apostle will allow no other source for the church than the cross of Jesus.

In a profound sense, the arms of Christ spreadeagled on the cross in his final agony become a fitting symbol of his sacrifice's achievement. With one outstretched arm he grasps believing Israelites, and with the other he grasps believing Gentiles; and, in his person offered up in holy oblation, he unites the two. Accordingly, 'he himself is our peace, who has made the two one' (Eph. 2:14). By his death, Christ Jesus (= Messiah Jesus, 2:13) has 'destroyed' the barrier and removed the grounds of the hostility.

In essence he does this by fulfilling in himself the ceremonial law (2:15), and by bearing, in his propitiatory self-sacrifice, the implications before God of Jewish and Gentile breaches of the moral law (2:16). Hence he 'put to death their hostility' (2:16b).

> O love of God, O sin of man,
> In this dread deed your strength is tried;
> And victory remains with love:
> Jesus my Lord is crucified![7]

The commentators have wrestled with the question of whether the 'hostility' here is the same as that referred to earlier, in verse 14: the *horizontal* enmity that existed between Jew and Gentile. Or, alternatively, is it the *vertical* 'hostility' which exists between God and humanity on account of our sinful rebellion against him (verse 16a)? There is much to be said, both grammatically and in the light of other Pauline passages on the achievement of the cross, for seeing *both* dimensions present.[8] In his death Christ *does things*; 'While our death is our fate, his death is his deed.'[9]

### A second dimension of the atonement

The cross in Ephesians 2 is seen to have a double effect: it removes both the wrath of God and the hostility of humans. That is, it creates a new, reconciled humanity: reconciled with God, and reconciled within itself. Hence we need to understand Paul as claiming that the cross *actually creates community*. This second dimension is regularly overlooked, and yet it is overwhelmingly important. By providing the one sufficient means whereby sin can be forgiven, Christ's death eliminates in principle all the religious distinctions between Jew and Gentile, with their inherent potential for pride and enmity.

But in so doing it also reaches to the core heart-attitudes that find expression in these specific forms of mutual antipathy. It does so by assaulting the fallen attitudes of unlove which inform so much of human relationships, including those under consideration in Ephesians chapter 2. It makes us people with an inherent instinct for love. That is, it actually creates, brings into being in space and time, a 'new humanity'.

### A 'third race': a new humanity

The second-century *Letter to Diogenes* (1.1) actually refers to Christians as a 'third race', distinct from Israel and the Gentiles. 'It is not that Gentiles become Jews (as Gentile proselytes did in pre-NT times), nor that Jews become Gentiles, but both become "one new person ... a whole new entity ... a new race which is raceless".'[10] Here is the great Ephesian image of the church. It is a new humanity, a community consisting of people remade. This is, I believe, the supreme image for our time, both for the church universal and for the church local.

The apostle's language here must not be diluted. He is asserting nothing less than a *sheer creative action of God*.[11] Just as, in his deed of creation, God spoke and the universe sprang into being, so now he speaks in his deed of redemption, and a new humanity leaps into existence. In 3:6, Paul refers to the new reality of Jews and Gentiles together under Christ as 'this mystery', something previously hidden but now divinely revealed. The creation of the church is accordingly a prodigy, a wonder, brought about by a supernatural, divine intervention, and hence a divine attestation to the gospel.[12]

### Much more than race

But what is being contemplated here is vastly more than a racial reconciliation. That such is included, and that in the first-century context it was in itself a highly impressive expression of this new humanity, is not to be doubted. But the 'newness' is vastly wider and deeper, involving a fundamental reconstitution of human relatedness, and hence inclusive of every primary form of interpersonal alienation. We shall attempt to provide biblical and theological justification of this claim in the following chapters; but the depth of the challenge to the relational life of Christian communities needs to be grasped at the outset: we belong together, in a new humanity with *all* the people of God.

This 'new order', this 'third race', this new humanity, is filled out in three vivid images, each expressing the sheer privilege of this new status. The first is political: 'you are ... fellow-citizens with God's people'. The second is familial: 'you are ... members of God's household'. The third is sacral: 'you are ... being built together to become a dwelling in which God lives by his Spirit' (2:19–22).[13]

> The Church is a new creation ... the 'new person', a new humanity
> included in Christ as the representative human being, thereby
> constituting his body ... characterized above all ... by its unity ...
> The Church is where men and women experience a sense of being at
> home, or belonging, not only to one another in a unified humanity as
> fellow citizens, but also to God himself as part of his household or
> family ... made into his dwelling place.[14]

### Heaven too!

In 3:10, during his inspired biographical digression (3:1–13), Paul unveils a remarkable further dimension of this new creation in Christ. Ephesians contains a whole series of references to 'the heavenly places' (1:3, 10, 20; 2:6; 3:10; 4:10; 6:12). Reality, for Paul, clearly transcends the earthly order. God's purpose in the church has supra-terrestrial trajectories. 'His intent was that now, through the church, the manifold wisdom of God should be made known to the rulers and authorities in the heavenly realms' (3:10).

But what does the church disclose to the heavenly powers? What makes the church 'a graduate school for angels'?[15] It is the 'mystery' whereby 'through the gospel the Gentiles are heirs together with Israel, members of one body, and sharers together in the promise in Christ Jesus' (3:6). It is the emergence of the astonishing 'diversity in unity' whereby Jews and Gentiles are brought together into a single new humanity as a foretaste of God's universal purpose, 'to bring all things together ... under one head, even Christ' (1:10). 'The church thus appears as God's pilot scheme for the reconciled universe of the future. The uniting of Jews and Gentiles was ... God's masterpiece of reconciliation, and gave promise of a time when *not Jews and Gentiles only, but all mutually hostile elements in creation* would be united in that same Christ.'[16]

Hence the union of Jew and Gentile, the theme of Ephesians 2:11–22, must be understood as only the paradigm expression of something much larger and more comprehensive – the body of Christ on earth, a unique God-created reality, a new humanity, in which not only racial diversity but every other major human diversity is both confronted and overcome.

### So what?

Thus, in summary, while the eternal purpose of God for the world and all its peoples, as well as for the denizens of the heavenly orders, is hidden from the unbelieving world, at two points it breaks through into visibility: first, the resurrection of Christ, and, second, the unifying, in a new, supernatural order of existence, of all those who acknowledge his rule – a new humanity in which, as in the resurrection, we see God's unveiled face and touch his outstretched hand.

### The 'Ephesian Moment'

Not that all this was immediately perceived, or universally practised, by the first Christian generation. Not surprisingly, the older diversities continued to live on for a period (cf. Acts 21:20–26). But the principle had been irrevocably established – the 'Ephesian Moment', as Andrew Walls calls it, had arrived for ever – and its greatest day, I believe, is about to dawn.[17]

The implications for our thinking about and planning for the church are, accordingly, major ones. Specifically, we are here afforded a congregational model that can be succinctly defined as 'diversity in unity under Christ'. It is a model that achieves two great goals. Firstly, it means building churches that move in the direction of God's purpose for the ages – all things together under Christ – and accordingly that self-consciously set out to unite in Christ the diversities and polarities of their surrounding communities.

Secondly, by virtue of this, it is a plan for congregational life that is profoundly doxological, one which glorifies God. This is exactly Paul's own response to it, in the remarkable prayer recorded in 3:14–21, ending in an outburst of praise which unsurprisingly links the glorifying of God to the twin elements of his eternal purpose – 'the church', the body in which all diversities are reconciled, and 'Christ', the exalted reconciler:

> Now to him who is able to do immeasurably more than all we ask or imagine ... to him be glory in the church and in Christ Jesus throughout all generations, for ever and ever! Amen.

Amen, indeed!

### Only a paradigm?

The case for the union of Jew and Gentile in Christ, clearly made from Ephesians 2, has been claimed as only a paradigm instance of the creation of a much wider human reconciliation. It is time now to justify this claim by widening our biblical base to include other New Testament evidence, and thus attempting to make good our contention that the calling of every local church, everywhere, if it is to be faithful to its New Testament roots, is, among other things, to be a community of reconciliation in which all the primary divisions and polarities of its surrounding culture are confronted and find resolution under the gracious reign of the Lord Jesus Christ.

## 2 It's more than race

*Other major diversities overcome*

### The Gospels: the mind of Jesus

Does Jesus give us any clues about how he envisages life for his followers after the conclusion of his own ministry? Are there any anticipations of the new humanity, whether in his teaching or in other aspects of his ministry?

Jesus stands within the Old Testament tradition in its assumption that faith is corporate. People relate to God not merely as isolated individuals but within a community of faith. Hence one of his first acts as he sets out on his mission is to call a group of disciples. 'He appointed twelve – designating them apostles – that they might be with him, and that he might send them out to preach' (Mark 3:14; cf. Luke 22:28–30). Jesus clearly anticipates a profound community experience for his disciples: 'I will build my church' (Matt. 16:18; cf. 18:17; 28:19–20; Luke 22:17–20; John 10:1–16; 13:2–17; 17:6–26).

#### Who gets in?

As to the place of the Gentiles in the new era of God's kingdom, the evidence, at first reading, is ambiguous. The disciples on their initial 'training' mission are told: 'Do not go among the Gentiles or enter any town of the Samaritans. Go rather to the lost sheep of Israel' (Matt. 10:5–6). In similar vein, the Canaanite mother pleading for her daughter's health is apparently rebuffed in the coinage of popular Jewish partisanship: 'I was sent only to the lost sheep of Israel ... It is not right to take the children's bread and toss it to their dogs' (Matt. 15:24, 26). In Matt. 23:15 Jesus even indicates his lack of enthusiasm for the current missionary activities of 'the teachers of the law and Pharisees', which aimed at recruiting new converts to Judaism among the Gentile nations.

In making sense of this, the time sequence is important. The period of Jesus' preaching and healing ministry belongs still within the time of anticipation: 'the Kingdom is at hand, but the time of its (full) revelation is yet to come'.[1] The kingdom can truly come only after the blood of the Passover Lamb has been shed (Isa. 53:1–12; Mark 10:45; 14:24; Luke 12:49–50; John 1:30; 8:28; 12:30–33).

Even within Jesus' preaching, however, there are clear anticipations of a wider mission perspective which includes the Gentiles, a perspective for which his place of upbringing had prepared him. For Jesus was raised in 'Galilee of the Gentiles' (Matt. 4:12–16).[2] We note in this regard his saying that 'the gospel must first be preached to all nations' and that 'the gospel is preached throughout the world' (Mark 13:10; 14:9). The disciple community is to be 'the light of the world' and 'the salt of the earth' (Matt. 5:13–14), reflecting the prophetic picture of the city of God, whose brightness, the glory of God, summons all the nations (Matt. 5:14; Isa. 42:6; 49:6). The final drama of history is expressed as a wedding feast, to which 'anyone you find' is welcomed (Matt. 22:9; cf. 22:1–14; 24:14, 31; Luke 14:23). Jesus also promises Gentiles a share in salvation (cf. Matt. 8:10–11; 12:41–42; 25:31–32). And, as Jesus' ministry reaches its Good Friday climax, he declares: 'I, when I am lifted up from the earth, will draw all people to myself' (John 12:32).

Critically, in his depiction of the final judgment, Jesus eliminates any reference to a distinction between Jew and Gentile (cf. Matt. 12:41–42; Mark 13:26–27; Luke 4:25–27; 13:1–5). Further, in referring to the Old Testament promises concerning the end of history, Jesus detaches the element of divine vengeance on the Gentile nations. 'The storm of protest in the synagogues at Nazareth during Jesus' preaching should in all probability be ascribed to the fact that he had dared to omit any reference to "the day of vengeance of our God" (Luke 4:17–19; cf. Isa. 61:1–2).'[3]

There is additionally the universalism, anticipated in the visit of the magi at his birth (Matt. 2:1–12), and expressed unequivocally in the scope of the Great Commission issued after his death: 'Go and make disciples of *all nations*' (Matt. 28:19, my italics; cf. Mark 16:15; Luke 24:47; Acts 1:8).

In reconciling the apparent contrast expressed in these two mission visions, we need to note a certain 'order', according to which the kingdom must be first offered to Israel. This reflects God's faithfulness to his covenant promises to them; though even there the universal scope of God's purpose is clear from the beginning: 'All peoples on earth will be blessed through you [Abraham]' (Gen. 12:3; also 15:5; 17:5).

This order continues to be reflected later in the apostolic mission, not least that of Paul, in Acts 13:46 for example, where the author of Ephesians 2:11–22 says to the Jews in Pisidian Antioch, 'We had to speak the word of God to you first' (cf. Acts 1:8; 10:1 – 11:18; Gal. 2:7). It is difficult to believe that this sense of priority did not stem originally from Jesus. The final goal, however, is always universal, as we noted, in the terms of the foundational covenant with Abraham (Gen. 12:3). 'The whole history of Israel is nothing but the continuation of the Lord's dealings with the nations.'[4]

### 'My house . . . for all nations'

Possibly the most significant pointer to Jesus' racially inclusive vision for the future of his community are his words and action in the holy shrine of Judaism, the Jerusalem Temple, at the close of his ministry.[5] Jesus authenticates his dramatic 'cleansing' action by appeal to Isaiah 56:7: 'Is it not written: "My house will be called a house of prayer *for all nations*"?' (Mark 11:17, my italics).

It was this last phrase, with its radical qualification of the divide between Jew and Gentile, that incensed the Jewish authorities and stoked the fires of their determination to kill him. 'In the Gospel of Mark (as graphically illustrated in this incident) Jesus is a preacher of multicultural worship. He envisioned a future which was radically different from the one espoused by the temple leadership.'[6]

Thus the dawn of the new age of the kingdom at Pentecost exhibits a significant muting of nationalistic vision (Acts 2:8–11) and presses irresistibly forward to the explicit inclusion of Gentiles (Acts 8 – 13). This entire development takes place with a naturalness that underlines its entire congruence with the vision and message of Jesus.

## Moved with compassion

But that congruence derives from another critical feature of the ministry of Jesus – his inclusive compassion, his uninhibited love towards all who would open themselves to God's word through him, irrespective of their national, moral or generational status. Hence, 'My command is this: *Love* each other *as I have loved* you' (John 15:12, my italics; cf. 13:14–15).

In particular, we note the way Jesus' love is directed towards the marginalized and outcast – to the person who is different from ourselves. Indeed, 'If you love [only] those who love you, what reward will you get? Are not even the tax collectors doing that? And if you greet only your own people, what are you doing more than others? Do not even pagans do that?' 'I tell you: Love your enemies and pray for those who persecute you, that you may be children of your Father in heaven' (Matt. 5:46–47, 44–45).

Here we encounter what is arguably among the supreme distinctions of Jesus' message and ministry, and hence a cardinal feature of the kingdom whose coming he announced. In Matthew 11:1–6 Jesus enumerates the signs of the kingdom's arrival, and pronounces the blessedness of those who are not offended thereby. The first five signs would have elicited no offence: the blind receive sight, the lame now walk, the lepers are healed, the deaf are given hearing, and the dead are raised. The crunch, however, lies in the final category: 'and the good news is preached to the poor' (Matt. 11:5; Luke 6:20). Here was the scandal; here lay the offence.

Who are the 'poor'? 'They are repeatedly called "publicans and sinners" (Matt. 11:19; Mark 2:16; Luke 15:1), "publicans and prostitutes" (Matt. 21:32), or simply "sinners" (Mark 2:17; Luke 7:37, 39; 15:2; 19:7) . . . It was a fairly general designation for those who notoriously failed to observe the commandments of God, and at whom, therefore, everyone pointed a finger.'[7]

Further, Jesus' followers were designated 'the little ones' (Mark 9:42; Matt. 10:42; 18:10, 14), 'the least' (Matt. 25:40, 45), or the 'simple ones' (Matt. 11:25), who are contrasted with the 'wise and understanding'.

'The disciples of Jesus are here designated as uneducated, backward and ... irreligious ... Jesus' following consisted predominantly of the disreputable ... the uneducated, whose religious ignorance and moral behaviour stood in the way of their access to salvation, according to the convictions of the time.'[8]

Jesus' welcome to the marginalized is also scandalously demonstrated in his offering these outcasts table-fellowship. Luke 15:2 has Jesus inviting them to his house, and reclining at table with them (Mark 2:15ff.). In the East, even today, to invite someone to a meal is an honour. 'It was an offer of peace, trust, brotherhood and forgiveness; in short, sharing a table meant sharing a life.'[9]

> It would be impossible to overestimate the impact these meals must
> have had upon the poor and the sinners. By accepting them as friends
> and equals Jesus had taken away their shame, humiliation and guilt.
> By showing them that they mattered to him as people he gave them
> a sense of dignity and released them from captivity. The physical
> contact which he must have had with them when reclining at the table,
> and which he obviously never dreamed of disallowing, must have made
> them feel clean and acceptable.[10]

In this light we can well understand the taunts, 'A glutton and a drunkard, a friend of tax collectors and "sinners"' (Matt. 11:19; Luke 7:34).

As a particular expression of this inclusive, gracious love, Jesus welcomed women and children. In Judaism women were in every sense the 'second sex'. This was confirmed in all manner of social customs and in the dictates of law. Josephus expressed the common opinion when he wrote: 'A woman is in every respect inferior to a man.'[11]

### Women...

As in many Islamic cultures today, morality was to be safeguarded by keeping women in seclusion. By contrast, Jesus speaks openly with a woman, so that his disciples are amazed (John 4:27). Women people his audiences (e.g. Luke 11:27). He is the friend of the sisters Mary and Martha (Luke 10:38–42; John 11 *passim*). Women are among his followers and support him out of their resources (Mark 15:40–41; Luke 8:1–3). 'This must have caused quite a sensation.'[12]

### ... and children

In the case of children, their status according to religious law is caught in the regularly occurring triadic phrase, 'the deaf and dumb, weak-minded, and under age'. Again, in the world of Jesus, the children, like the women, counted of little value. Jesus openly and pointedly receives them and extends his blessing to them (Mark 10:13–16). Jesus puts them in the context of salvation (Mark 10:14), and speaks of the need to identify with them to be saved (Matt. 18:3). The child is in fact the model disciple (Mark 9:33–37).

Thus Jesus, both by his teaching and by his actions, constituted the body of his followers as an inclusive community which was open to those who were different, a community which was emphatically *not* confined to the 'people like us who make us feel comfortable'. Specifically, his community was to be characterized by the welcome into its life and activity of those whom surrounding society regarded with suspicion and passed under judgment.

### '... and de walls came a-tumblin' down'?

It is impossible to ignore the challenge of this clear finding from the Gospels. We have no mandate to gather Christian communities, claiming Jesus' name, that are surrounded by walls of exclusivity, whether of race, colour or ethnicity, gender, age or generation, social or economic status, mental and physical well-being; or communities entirely confined to those who come with impeccable histories of moral and spiritual propriety. The community that Jesus formed, and then called his disciples to emulate in their subsequent ministry, was emphatically inclusive of those who did not, initially at least, share the disciples' convictions, lifestyle or values.

This is not to imply, of course, any muting of the call to repentance and godly living, or of the urgent summons to receive Jesus Christ as Saviour and Lord. The critical distinction, signalled in baptism, between those who embrace God's salvation in Christ and those who do not can never be reduced. But the godly life is also the love-filled life, after the pattern of Jesus here, which will imply our offering to every human neighbour an instinctive welcome, expressed in genuine respect and loving compassion.

There is a major integrity issue here for many local churches. In what sense is Jesus Lord of our life together? Can we honestly claim his name and blessing when our communal life is carefully encircled by walls of exclusivism? Putting this another way, who is the Jesus we claim as Lord and seek to please and serve? If he is not the Jesus of the Gospels, who is he? Is there any other Jesus?

This glance at Jesus in the Gospels prepares us for an examination of the earliest Christian congregations which were the direct successors of the disciple community of Jesus.

## THE LETTERS: THE MIND OF THE APOSTLES

### Galatians 3:26–28

The background to the deeply passionate letter to the Galatians, arguably the first piece of the New Testament to be written, is neatly registered in Acts 15:1: 'Certain individuals came down from Judea to Antioch, and were teaching the believers: "Unless you are circumcised, according to the custom taught by Moses, you cannot be saved." ' These very teachers, or others identically persuaded, had visited the Galatian churches, and a significant number of the believers there had begun to buy into their Jewish Christian version of the gospel, 'which is really no gospel at all' (Gal. 1:7).

### A curse for us

In response to these legalistic revisionists (whom Peterson in *The Message* aptly designates 'the lawmen'), Paul argues that our acceptance with God lies *solely* in Christ's atoning sacrifice on the cross (Gal. 3:13). There he bore our 'curse', the divine judgment that follows inevitably upon all breaches of the divine law (3:10; cf. Deut. 27:1; 28:1). He bore it by becoming, himself, 'a curse for us' in the terms of Deuteronomy 21:23, a provision in the Old Testament law whereby criminals who had committed offences requiring removal from the covenant community were exposed on a tree following execution. This was done in token of their having become the object of divine judgment, that is, being under the curse of God.

Astonishingly, Paul sees this operating at the cross. There, in the incredible wonder of God's love and justice, God in Christ, the innocent, took the place of the guilty, bearing their judgment on their behalf, and thereby releasing them from its penalty. 'Christ died for sins once for all, the just for the unjust, to bring you to God' (1 Pet. 3:18).

Luther's stirring prose still resonates:

> Our merciful Father, seeing us to be oppressed and overwhelmed with the curse of the law, and to be so holden down by the same that we could never be delivered by our own power, sent his only Son into the world and laid upon him the sins of all men, saying: be thou Peter that denier; Paul that persecutor; David that adulterer; that sinner which did eat the apple in Paradise; that thief which hanged upon the cross; and briefly, be thou the person which hath committed the sins of all men; see therefore that thou pay and satisfy for them.[13]

As far as the attainment of a righteous status before God is concerned, nothing can be added to this from the human perspective, whether rites such as circumcision, or other acts of ceremonial observance; not even general moral rule-keeping. The road being advocated by the Galatian legalists is a road to disaster. It is the abrogation of the gospel of grace, the impossible demand for self-salvation, and hence a return to spiritual enslavement and to resultant final condemnation. Salvation by grace through the cross – that, and that alone – is the gospel authorized by divine revelation, the gospel the Galatians had received, and which alone could maintain their standing with God. The message of the 'lawmen' must be rejected unequivocally.

However, God's act of sheer mercy, whereby Christ died for us (that is, *God in Christ*), is not an end in itself, nor a solely personal deliverance. It is, rather, a means to the fulfilment of God's eternal, communal purpose of grace. It happened 'in order that the blessing given to Abraham might come to the Gentiles through Christ (Messiah) Jesus, so that by faith we might receive the promise of the Spirit' (Gal. 3:14). The 'promise of the Spirit' is our participation in the new life of the kingdom of God, the end-time, eschatological blessing, promised to Israel in the Old Testament and now present in the Holy Spirit. Thus, the faith that justifies is a faith that simultaneously regenerates by inserting us into the body of Christ, the family of God, the new community of the kingdom (3:26 – 4:7). By our faith-baptism we are united to Christ, 'baptised into Christ ... clothed ... with Christ ... Abraham's seed, and heirs according to the promise' (3:27–29). We belong to a new humanity.

### All one

The unpacking of that is in a much-discussed verse, 3:28: 'There is now [for all who were baptized into Christ, verse 27] neither Jew nor Greek, slave nor free, male nor female, for you are all one in Christ Jesus.'

The debates have centred on the final couplet, referring to gender difference, and its implications for the struggle for female equality in culture generally, and within Christian culture particularly. Our concern is with the larger perspective of the text as a whole. Clearly, for Paul, becoming a Christian means living in a new world. The key words are 'Before ... Now' (23, 25). How are we to characterize this new order? Specifically, it means a relativizing of former distinctions, and the creation of a new unity of life that transcends them.

Three relationships are noted, covering 'the fundamental cleavages of human existence'. Race / ethnicity, socio-political status, and gender; all these have been impacted by the gospel of grace.[14]

The first relationship, between Jews and Gentiles, we have addressed above in examining Paul's later statement in Ephesians 2:11–22. It was an obvious category within Paul's Galatian argument also. The Judaistic revisionists, by their insistence on circumcision and law-keeping, were in effect endlessly prolonging the racial distinction between Jew and Gentile. In the light of Christ's sacrifice on behalf of all people, irrespective of their race or ethnicity, such distinctions are rendered void. All the redeemed, whether Jew or Gentile in their pre-Christian lives, come to God, and are established as his children, by their faith in the cross-work of Christ, and by that alone. Hence 'there is neither Jew nor Greek [Gentile]'. The new humanity in Christ knows no racial or ethnic distinction.

### Slavery under fire

'Neither slave nor free' touches one of the fundamentals of Greco-Roman social order. In Greek and Roman thought, slavery was a natural phenomenon, how life was given. Since only citizens were, strictly speaking, 'human', slaves were sub-human chattels. In practice, slaves were not uncommonly treated with some degree of humanity; none-theless, 'throughout classical antiquity the institution of slavery was taken for granted, even by those who worked for its amelioration'.[15]

The full extent of the practice within the first-century Roman Empire may have extended to a third of the population, particularly in Rome and the major metropolitan centres in the western empire. In Christ, slavery, too, has ceased to divide.

### Sister, not slave

In the year 203, in Carthage in North Africa, a young noblewoman, Perpetua, was won to Christ though her slave maid, Felicitas. Despite the poignant appeals of her family, Perpetua refused to recant and, along with Felicitas, was condemned 'to the beasts'. On the day of their martyrdom the two women walked calmly out into the arena hand in hand and, in that moment, in the name of Jesus Christ, slavery was effectively dead.

Embodied in that potent act of supreme courage was the announcement of a new way of existing, of being human, a new humanity. A new society had arrived in which the accidents of birth, and the oppressive denial of human rights, including the right to freedom, by military-backed political authorities, were all superseded. Here was a new order in which men, women and children were all equally free, and equally dignified, without consideration of how they might be viewed or treated within any given political or social milieu. 'In Christ ... there is neither slave nor free.'

### And gender too

The third expression of the new unity in Christ is Paul's claim that 'there is neither ... male nor female'. As is commonly noted, the Greek here is nuanced slightly and literally reads, 'there is neither male *and* female'. The difference almost certainly arises from the apostle's quoting from Genesis 1:27: 'So God created human beings in his own image ... male *and* female he created them.' The extension of his specification of the forms of new-humanity community to the gender distinction takes us to the most fundamental of all human distinctions, extending back, like no other, to the origin of the human story (Gen. 1:27–28; 2:18–25; 1 Cor. 11:11–12). Nothing could more clearly demonstrate the radical nature of the new relationships that stem from the achievement of the cross.

### Equals 'in Christ Jesus'

That there is a natural progression in the case of this third category of diversity in unity from the earlier Jew–Gentile relationship is largely overlooked by the commentators, and yet it appears obvious enough. The primary insistence of the 'lawmen' was on the need to be circumcised (Gal. 2:3, 12; 5:2–3, 6, 11–12; 6:15). Circumcision as practised in Judaism, however, was a gender-discriminatory rite, being performed only on males. Accordingly, the insistence on circumcision as a requirement for Christians, apart from destroying the graciousness and efficacy of the gospel, would also necessarily reassert the physiologically rooted gender distinction of the rite. Since only males were circumcised, and since that would continue to be the case in a Christianized form of circumcision, the gender distinction with its potentially discriminatory overtones would have been perpetuated in the church.

It is not beside the point that this statement in Galatians 3:28 is immediately preceded by a reference to baptism: 'all of you ... were baptised into Christ ... there is neither male nor female' (3:27–28).

The relationship between circumcision and baptism is a complex though important issue, and it lies beyond the scope of this book. Sufficient to note that the newness of the new covenant and the new humanity in Christ, as against the old order in Judaism, lies not least in the rites associated with entry into the respective communities, namely circumcision and baptism. Since baptism is practised identically in every respect in the case of women and men, one of its 'better things' is its unambiguous declaration that in Christ there is neither male nor female (cf. Acts 8:12; Heb. 11:40).[16]

But the prefacing of Galatians 3:28 by the reference to baptism is significant for a deeper reason. For in baptism, as Paul argues in Romans 6:1–11, is declared nothing less than a radical ending and a radically new beginning that can be adequately denoted only by death and resurrection from the dead.

### Dying and rising again

But this 'dying and rising' enshrined in Christian baptism is not only a picture of the new beginning in the baptized person's life (vividly enacted where the form used is immersion), but, in addition, a supernatural event in which the baptized is actually taken back into union with Christ, participating with him in the saving events of his death and resurrection in Jerusalem two thousand years ago. 'Don't you know that all of us who were baptised into Christ were baptised into his death? We were therefore buried with him through baptism into death in order that, just as Christ was raised from the dead through the glory of the Father, we too may live a new life' (Rom. 6:4; cf. Col. 2:12). Baptism so understood proclaims, as nothing else could, the cataclysmic gulf between the pre-Christian life and the 'life made new' in our faith-union in the Holy Spirit with the Lord Jesus Christ.

In the subsequent life of the Christian, even the most fundamental relationships are submitted accordingly to a transforming renewal. True, there is continuity. Racial and ethnic identity are not eliminated. The great host to be gathered around the throne of God in the revelation of the coming glory in Daniel 7 and Revelation 7 are still recognizable in their ethnic and racial identities, 'from every nation, tribe, people and language' (Rev. 7:9). Indeed, the Holy City that will come down from God will embrace the splendour of the nations (Rev. 21:24). Similarly, the gender distinction and natural family relation-ships remain as before (Eph. 5:21–33; Col. 3:18–21; 1 Pet. 3:1–7; Heb. 13:4). Nor, in respect of the social-status distinction of slavery or freedom, does Paul call directly for the elimination of all such from society (1 Cor. 7:20, 24), though where liberty can be obtained he encourages its being attained (1 Cor. 7:21–23).

But in essence the Christian is living as a new person in a new world, amid a new community in which *all* the old hostilities are 'put to death' in the cross, as it is embraced in baptism. The Christian experiences life in Christ as a life in which 'all are one' (3:28).

'These three couplets (Jew/Greek; slave/free; male/female) also cover in embryonic fashion all the essential relationships of humanity, and so need to be seen as having racial, cultural, and sexual implic-ations as well.'[17] Thus our claim when examining Ephesians 2:11–22, that the 'putting to death' of the old hostility between Jew and Gentile was only a paradigm instance of a vastly more comprehensive unity, is clearly vindicated here.

## Colossians 3:10–11

Colossians, like Ephesians, with which it exhibits significant parallels, is another of Paul's prison letters. The background was ostensibly a prison visit by Epaphras, who had founded a church in Colosse, a small community in the Lycus valley, some time during Paul's great third journey (Acts 18:23 – 21:16). The congregation was being affected by a 'new theology' that Epaphras recognized as inimical to the truth of the gospel, but a deviation he was probably not competent to deal with himself, and so he sought Paul's help. The result is this letter to the Colossians.

The flawed 'gospel' circulating in Colosse has to be deduced from Paul's treatment of it, but essentially, not unlike the Galatian heresy, it was offering Christians a 'Christ plus' message, a fuller 'truth' than the 'simple' (!) gospel of salvation by faith in Christ. This 'philosophy' (2:8) claimed to impart a greater knowledge (2:18, 23), and a personal fullness of life (1:19, 25; 2:9–10) to its initiates. The road to this spiritual nirvana lay in faith in Christ *supplemented* by a specific amalgam of Jewish and pagan religious practices. The former appear in references to food regulations, Sabbath and other calendar observances, and probably, once again, circumcision (2:11–18). The latter was expressed in appeals for abstinence and severe asceticism (2:21–23), and the need to placate powerful unseen spiritual agencies and angelic mediators (1:16; 2:10, 15, 18).

### Christ is enough!

Paul's essential treatment is to remind the Colossians (and us) that we already possess more than we can ever need in Jesus Christ and in our union with him in his death and rising (1:15–20; 2:2–3; 2:9 – 3:4). Through our faith-participation in Christ, sealed in our baptism, we have been brought into a radically new kind of existence, a 'new self' (3:10) or a new humanity. Belonging to this order, we have no need to supplement our relationship with Christ by the strict observance of either Old Testament laws or other extrabiblical religious practices. Indeed, to claim the need for such is to undermine our standing in grace.

In the concluding section of the letter, Paul builds on the foundation of our glorious new humanity in Christ by noting that this carries with it certain moral and behavioural obligations. At the *individual* level, it calls for dying to the old order of life, putting off the old self (3:5, 9), by renouncing sexual vices (3:5), and antisocial attitudes and conduct (3:8–9). But there are *communal* implications also, for the 'new self' is corporate as well as individual, in correspondence to the Christ who is both the personal image of God *and* the one to whom those who believe in him are being corporately conformed (1:15; 3:10–11).

### New self, new family

The communal implications are spelled out: 'Here there is no Greek or Jew, circumcised or uncircumcised, barbarian, Scythian, slave or free, but Christ is all, and is in all' (3:11). Once more, the Christian's new life in union with Christ overreaches natural divisions, and once more these are unpacked in specific detail, which goes beyond the ethnic and racial and so removes any doubt concerning their universal range. The new humanity calls for a whole new world of human relatedness.

Paul mentions the Jew/Gentile divide first and employs a double reference, 'no Greek' (the outstanding representatives of Gentiles) 'or Jew, circumcised or uncircumcised'. This starting point is entirely to be expected when a significant part of the Colossian heresy called for believers to submit to specific features of the Old Testament law, including, in all probability, the rite of circumcision.[18]

The list then moves from religious prejudice to cultural and class prejudice. This division is perhaps already present in the use of the term 'Greeks', in whose eyes all who were unable to speak their language were irredeemably uncultured and hence contemptible 'barbarians'. Among this latter class none were more debased than the 'Scythians', from the northern reaches of Asia, 'little better than wild beasts', according to Josephus. 'The ancient world, just like the modern, was an elaborate network of prejudice, suspicion and arrogance, so ingrained as to be thought natural and normal.'[19]

This focus on social divisions leads naturally to the final couplet, 'slave or free'. A little later Paul will memorably expound the ways in which the new communal identity in Christ has essentially eliminated, for Christians concerned, the distinction between slave and master. 'Slaves, obey your earthly masters ... not only when their eye is on you ... Whatever you do, work at it with all your heart, as working for the Lord, not for human masters ... It is the Lord Christ you are serving ... there is no favouritism. Masters, provide your slaves with what is right and fair, because you know that you also have a Master in heaven' (3:22 – 4:1).

### Christ in all

The entire series in verse 11 is neatly bracketed by the theological reality, which is both the basis of this radical relativization of social divisions, and also the pattern to which the new-humanity relationships are being conformed: 'being renewed in knowledge in the image of the Creator' (3:10), and 'Christ is all, and is in all' (3:11). 'The image of the Creator' is finally, as 1:15 states, Christ himself. As such, Christ is the one by whom all things were created, including all humanity (1:16); Christ is the one in whom all things hold together, including all humanity (1:17); Christ is the one for whom all things were created, including all humanity (1:16). He is the source, the sustainer and the goal of all human existence. Hence 'Christ himself amounts to everything' (3:11).[20]

Beside this cosmic Christ all human distinctions are simply relativized into secondary significance, before the one whose powerful efficacy, in solidarity with his human creatures (1:22), will finally restore to all his people humanity's primal image of God. 'Only a Christology as fully insistent as Paul's on both the divinity and humanity of Jesus Christ can undergird this claim, that in him there can be no barriers between human beings.'[21]

Further, and finally, 'Christ is *in* all'. Salvation means incorporation into a unity of life with the one who died and rose again (2:11–15, 20; 3:1–4). It means a degree of identification such that 'Christ is your life' (3:4), a life 'now hidden with Christ in God' (3:3). Hence we cannot consider a Christian other than as a man or woman 'in Christ' (2 Cor. 12:2). Jesus had anticipated this amazing reality in his teaching: 'I am the vine; you are the branches' (John 15:5); 'Anyone who receives you receives me' (Matt. 10:40; cf. 25:40; John 13:20).

This glorious truth, which broke forcibly upon Paul's consciousness outside Damascus – 'Saul, Saul, why do you persecute *me*?' (Acts 9:4, my italics) – became enshrined in his image of the church as 'the body of Christ', and central to his understanding of Christian discipleship. Here is the ultimate ground for the loving mutuality of Christian people. Christ indwells every brother and every sister, no matter their social status, cultural instinct or religious heritage. To reject a fellow believer is to reject Christ. Correspondingly, to be brought by God's sovereign mercy into the life of the new humanity is to be obligated to live out a communal experience in which there are no second-class people, in which *all* the divisions of the surrounding culture fall under the feet of our crucified, risen and reigning Lord.

## 1 Corinthians 12:1–30

The divisions in Corinth were proverbial, and hence a timely reminder that the new humanity is always an enterprise 'in progress' on this side of the return of Christ. The presenting point of tension here was apparently the exercise of spiritual gifts, especially the more overtly charismatic ones, and their implications for good and godly order in worship.

### One in the Spirit

Again we are reminded of the reign of Christ: 'There are different kinds of service, but the same Lord' (12:5). Once again the new humanity transcends diversity and its attendant potential for conflict, in this case around gifts and ministries, and, perhaps underlying these, diversities of personality within a local congregation reflected also in the hero-worshipping of different Christian leaders (1:12; 3:21–22).

'Spirits' do need to be tested (1 John 4:1; 1 Thess. 5:21). Not everything that claims to be from God is from God. That was so in the earliest days of the church, and it remains so.

Paul offers some significant 'tests' of authentic Spirit ministries in this letter. True Holy Spirit gifts acknowledge that 'Jesus is Lord' and exalt him (12:3). True Holy Spirit gifts are used 'for the common good' of the congregation (12:7). True Holy Spirit gifts operate as consciously part of a 'body of Christ' ministry, and hence within a conscious affirmation of all other gifts of a congregation (12:11–27). True Holy Spirit gifts produce 'strengthening, encouragement and comfort' in a congregation (14:3). True Holy Spirit gifts seek, not the self-edification of the member concerned, but the edification of the church concerned (14:4–5). True Holy Spirit gifts aim to 'build up the church' (14:12). True Holy Spirit gifts value intelligibility (14:6–25). True Holy

Spirit gifts pursue 'peace . . . fittingness and order' (14:33, 40). Above all, true Holy Spirit gifts will, in being exercised, embody the Spirit's supreme gift, that of love (12:31 – 13:13).

However, while the Spirit's ministries are to be tested, they are also not to be summarily dismissed: 'Do not put out the Spirit's fire' (1 Thess. 5:19). We cannot forget Paul's own acknowledgment, 'I thank God that I speak in tongues more than all of you' (14:18), or his assertion that 'the kingdom of God is not a matter of talk but of power' (4:20).

### Belonging together

Rather, Paul does two things. Firstly, he reminds them again of their unity in Christ (12:4–6, 11–13, 24–26); they are 'all baptised by the one Spirit into one body' (12:13). They are one new humanity and are to live that out. Secondly, he commends to them the best 'fruit' of the Spirit, love, in terms that have remained the gold standard for human relationships through twenty centuries (13:1–13).[22]

The general point to be noted here for our overall new-humanity theme is that, despite the tensions created by the misuse of the Spirit's gifts and ministries on the part of some, there is not even a suggestion, on Paul's part, of the congregation dividing into separately worshipping 'sets', for the 'charismatically hot' and the 'charismatically cool' respectively. Once again, the unity in Christ ('we were all baptised by one Spirit into one body – whether Jews or Greeks, slave or free – and we were all given the one Spirit to drink'; 12:13) means that diversity is to be faced and embraced, rather than feared and fled from.

### 1 John 2:12–14

This passage, in which John addresses his new-humanity readers with typical pastoral concern, employs a threefold division within the congregation(s): 'little' or 'dear children' (12, 13); 'fathers' (13, 14); and 'young men' (13, 14). This literary unit in the letter continues to puzzle interpreters. 'No one has advanced a satisfactory explanation of the role of 2:12–14 within the body of 1 John.'[23]

My comments are therefore necessarily tentative, but I believe that seeing the three categories as a straightforward reference to three generations within the church is most worthy of consideration. At the very least, this passage confirms the impression conveyed elsewhere that the congregations in the first century were no less inclusive in their age-span than ours today (Acts 2:17; 6:1; 9:39; 10:24; 12:13; 16:1, 16, 31–33; 20:9; 21:5, 9; 23:16), and that the insistent appeal of this letter to mutual love after the pattern of the self-giving love of Christ (cf. 1 John 4:19, 'We love because he first loved us') had reference to generational distinctions as surely as to any others.

### 'Men and women of ripe old age ... boys and girls playing'

This multi-generational community is powerfully asserted in Acts 2, where Peter's citation of Joel's prophecy concerning the new era of the outpoured Spirit focuses its generational inclusivity: 'Your sons and daughters will prophesy; your young men will see visions, your old men will dream dreams' (Acts 2:17). One could cite other messianic anticipations to similar effect, along with Jesus' estimate of the spiritual ministry of children (Ps. 8:2; Isa. 11:1–9; 40:11; 49:22–23; 54:13; 65:20–25; Jer. 31:11–14; Joel 2:28; Matt. 21:14–16; Mark 9:36–39; 10:13–16). Nor can we fail to resonate with the beautiful picture in Zechariah 8:4–5 of God's outpoured blessing in its multi-generational expression: 'Once again men and women of ripe old age will sit in the streets of Jerusalem, each with cane in hand ... The city streets will be filled with boys and girls playing there.'

So again the new humanity expresses itself in a visible fellowship in which diversity is transcended in a supernatural unity, centred in the person of Christ, who is 'the true God and eternal life' (1 John 5:20).

### Hebrews 12:22–23

This remarkable passage identifies a dimension of the unified life of the new humanity that is rarely focused, and yet is highly significant, not least in affording evidence of its essentially supernatural nature. The dimension in question is the unity of the present communities of faith with believers of previous eras, as well as with the angelic and other servants of God inhabiting the celestial order. Such is the plain meaning of this passage. We 'have come [in our worship] ... to thousands upon thousands of angels in joyful assembly ... and to the spirits of the righteous made perfect'.

## Joining worship

We get it wrong so often when we start the service by saying 'Let us begin worship with this song of praise, or hymn (etc.)'. Whether in personal worship or in corporate worship, we do not, we never, *'begin'* worship; we only *join* worship. There are few truths more encouraging to the spirit in times of spiritual dryness.

But this, too, is part of the new humanity, for, 'since Christ continues to be formed in local communities of his people, whose ways of life are quite different from those within which the incarnation took place, it means that "sacred time" extends to the entire historical span in which the work of salvation goes on.' Accordingly, 'Christian faith is necessarily ancestor conscious', not in the sense of divinizing the dead in Christ, but of recognizing that they actually, if mysteriously, continue to be part of the one body.[24]

This particular diversity is of a different order from those previously considered, but it is no less real, and in its way it is a critical reminder that, when we refer to the new-humanity congregation and the new quality of relational life that it reflects, we are talking about the irreducibly supernatural. This book rests entirely upon a belief in the reality of the living God and the accessibility of his Spirit. Apart from his presence and enabling, the new humanity is just one more ephemeral utopia as far as the realization of human community is concerned. Without God's enabling, we, no less than secular prognosticators, are reduced to silence regarding the prospects for the Christian church.

But the 'mystic, sweet communion' with the saints of earlier ages is also a further argument, in accord with the findings of our exploration of 1 John 2:12–14, against limiting our communal vision in the local church to a single generation. No single generation can enclose the church, because no single generation constitutes the church. Hence, not least, the value in worship of drawing upon the resources of the church of the ages, and the blessing of a conscious rootedness within the 'glorious company of the Apostles', the 'goodly fellowship of the Prophets' and the 'noble army of Martyrs', to say nothing of the 'holy Church throughout all the world', the 'Cherubin and Seraphin', and 'all Angels'.[25]

Thus our consideration of these didactic New Testament passages justifies the claim, made earlier, that the communal life of the followers of Jesus, which emerged from the church's evangelistic mission in the New Testament period, was a life in which *all* the principal spheres of diversity were transcended in a new, divinely given unity – the emergence, in other words, of a radically new kind of human connectedness.

## The book of Acts: some New Testament congregations

A third line of New Testament evidence is to be found in the descriptions within the book of Acts of the fledgling congregations that emerged in these first decades of the Christian movement. We stop by five of them.

### The Jerusalem church: Acts 2:1–47

Pentecost was many things, but central to this epochal moment was the communication of the gospel in a supernaturally generated diversity of tongues to the geographically scattered, proselyte audience, as 'Jews from every nation under heaven' (2:5) confessed in amazement: 'We hear them declaring the wonders of God in our own tongues!' (2:11).

#### The anti-Babel
Some commentators have noted a rabbinic tradition that makes similar claims for the giving of the law on Sinai. More likely is the link to Genesis 11:1–9. 'The event was surely nothing less than a reversal of the curse of Babel',[26] an association which, if valid, detaches the Pentecostal outpouring from its Jewish, first-century moorings, and positions it squarely within universal history. The offspring of Pentecost is nothing less than a global child. The new humanity on its birthday represents massive ethnic diversity embraced in a supernaturally generated unity. We compare here words of Jesus, citing Isaiah 56:7, with its end-time promise, 'My house will be called a house of prayer for *all nations*' (Mark 11:17, my italics).

#### Gender and generation
While the *racial* diversity in unity is clearly primary, we ought not to overlook two other dimensions alluded to in Acts 2. The first is *gender*

*diversity.* The account of the praying company upon whom the Spirit descended mentions 'the women and Mary the mother of Jesus' (1:14), and the description of the manifestations of the Spirit is notably inclusive: 'they were *all* together . . . tongues of fire . . . separated and came to rest up on *each of them . . . All of them* were filled with the Holy Spirit and began to speak in other tongues' (2:1–4, my italics). It would be surprising indeed if the women who are already noted as participants in the many-tongued proclamation had no part whatever in this public overflow, not least when Peter's justification of the phenomenon cites Joel 2:28–32, which explicitly states that 'Your sons *and daughters* will prophesy . . . Even on my servants, *both men and women*, I will pour out my Spirit in those days, and they will prophesy' (Acts 2:17–18, my italics).

The same citation also has pointers to another dimension of new-humanity diversity, the *generational*: 'your young men will see visions, your old men will dream dreams' (2:17).

The coming of the Spirit awakened a whole new sense of 'belonging together', a communal experience in which everybody was important and everyone had a contribution to offer. This was expressed in the most tangible manner by the spontaneous sharing of material resources. 'All the believers were together and had everything in common. Selling their possessions and goods, they gave to anyone who had need' (2:44–45; cf. 4:32).

But it also manifested itself in the inclusiveness of their acceptance of each other. Hence, what would have been unthinkable in Judaism now blossomed in Christianity, as the men and the women, the old and the young, were united in a heaven-born commonality of life in which the former hierarchies gave way to mutual respect and a true equality. 'All the believers were together . . . [they] were one in heart and mind' (2:44; 4:32), a unity flowing from their overwhelming consciousness of the enthronement of the risen Jesus: 'Exalted to the right hand of God, he has poured out what you now see and hear' (2:33).

### So what?

The most effective way to demonstrate the new paradigm of Pentecost is through the local congregation of the church. The consequences of Babel will continue as long as the church fails to deal with the calling of being a multicultural community. Linguistic and cultural differences will be reinforced. Many of our contemporaries are not going to be permanently drawn to Christ through bigger and more effective churches that are driven by the values of our culture. Instead the experience manifested and postulated in the New Testament needs to be recovered and modeled afresh . . . into the new millennium.[27]

## The church in Syrian Antioch: Acts 11:19–26

The persecution triggered by Stephen's death scattered the witnessing church. At Antioch the historic breakthrough was made as 'men from Cyprus and Cyrene' took the critical step – in its way as significant as the legendary 'one small step' by Neil Armstrong onto the surface of the moon on 20 July 1969: they 'began to speak to Greeks also, telling them the good news about the Lord Jesus' (11:20). 'The importance of this step can hardly be overestimated. Antioch was the third largest city in the world.'[28] 'Almost a microcosm of Roman antiquity in the first century, [Antioch] encompassed most of the advantages, the problems, and the human interests with which the new faith would have to grapple.'[29]

### Diversity in unity

The diversity of this Syrian congregation emerges in the description of the congregation's leadership team, five in number: Barnabas (from Cyprus); Simeon called Niger (= 'the Black') (an African); Lucius of Cyrene (a North African); Manaen (possibly a slave of Herod's father, a Palestinian Jew); and Saul of Tarsus (a native of Asia Minor, the land-bridge to Europe) (13:1). 'A more heterogeneous group could hardly be suggested.'[30]

Bakke cites the archaeological evidence that the city, not unlike Jerusalem of our own time, was divided into distinct ethnic sectors, separated by walls, in this case five in number: Greek, Syrian, Jewish, Latin and African.[31] Just as the coming of the gospel effectively destroyed the 'dividing wall of hostility' between Jew and Gentile, so it effectively destroyed the interior walls of Antioch to enable men, women and children from every sector to come together to hear the gospel and become followers of the 'Lord Jesus' (11:20).

It is also highly significant that it was here that the name 'Christian' began to be applied to the followers of Jesus (11:26) – a further critical indication of their sheer 'newness', but a newness, be it noted, expressed not least in the diversity of their community. The citizens of Antioch could find no serviceable term to refer to them, either within Judaism or in any other Gentile religious tradition. It was a new thing and required a new name, but one which identified it with its primary focus – the Lord Jesus Christ – and with its most obvious feature, its welcoming of *every* race and *every* type – hence 'Christ-ones', *Christians*. Is it too much to claim that we truly justify our right to the name 'Christian' only when we practise diversity in unity under Christ?

## The church in Philippi: Acts 16:11–40

The three founding members of the Philippian congregation are, in turn, first, Lydia, a well-to-do businesswoman from Thyatira (Acts 16:14), a city in the province of Asia, 'a dealer in purple cloth', for which that region was famed. (The Greek translated 'Lydia' is literally 'the Lydian woman'; she possibly had a personal name in addition.) Second, there was a formerly demonically possessed slave girl (16:16–18); and third, the chief administrator of the city prison (16:23–34).

The social diversity enclosed in this triad is simply staggering. There may in addition be an indication of a highly visible gender diversity if, as seems implied, 'Lydia' became a leader from the beginning (16:15–16, 40).

## The church in Corinth: Acts 18:1–18

The report in Acts 18 of Paul's evangelistic ministry in Corinth follows a typical pattern. First there was teaching in the synagogue to Jews and God-fearing Gentiles (18:4–5). This produced a nucleus of converts, including Titius Justus (Acts 18:7), and Stephanas and his household (1 Cor. 1:16; 16:15), who were all Gentiles; and Jews such as Crispus, the synagogue ruler, and his household (Acts 18:8; 1 Cor. 1:14). When persecution arose, Paul moved next door to Crispus' home, where 'the whole church' continued to meet. Since Corinth is generally agreed to be the most likely place of composition of the letter to the Romans, there are further evidences of the racial diversity there according to Romans 16:21, 23, mentioning Jews such as Lucius, Jason and Sosipater, and Gentiles such as Erastus and Quartus.

### All shapes and sizes

There is also evidence in Paul's first letter to the Corinthians that the majority of the congregation came from the lower strata of society: 'Not many of you were wise by human standards; not many were influential; not many were of noble birth' (1 Cor. 1:26). Evidently some were slaves (1 Cor. 7:21–24), while others were free. Paul's response is to argue that in Christ these distinctions are now irrelevant: 'those who were slaves when called by the Lord are the Lord's freed people; similarly, those who were free when called are Christ's slaves' (7:22). 'Since God had called the Corinthians into koinonia [fellowship] with his crucified Son, it was his fellowship, and not any status in the world, which determined their relationship to God' and hence their true status.[32]

Further, the Corinthian congregation reflected another major social diversity: marital status. Here, in one chapter, we meet the married (7:2–5, 10–11); the single, like Paul himself (7:7–8), including both those who wish to remain unmarried (7:6, 8, 37), whether women (7:25–26) or men (7:37–38), and those who would like to get married (7:9, 28, 36–38); the engaged (36); and the formerly married, whether as the result of divorce (15), or the death of a spouse (39). Again, in whichever status they are, all are to continue to love, accept and minister to each other within the one Christian family.

That tensions arose out of this new-humanity social mix is not in question. We can note, for example, the divisions over leaders (1:1–12), and around the *agapē* feast, apparently along economic lines (11:20–22). One could also cite the evidence of the division over the exercise of spiritual gifts noted earlier, and hence, to a degree, over spiritual maturity, and perhaps also over innate personality (1 Cor. 12 – 14).

The new humanity, as the Corinthian correspondence as a whole surely demonstrates, is always a pilgrim enterprise, on the way but not yet having arrived. Despite all these experienced tensions and polarities, however, Paul's counsel at no point contemplates the division of the church into separate worshipping groupings. The call is rather to a rediscovery of the Holy Spirit's supreme gift of love, which is patient and kind, which does not envy or boast, and which is not proud, rude, self-seeking or easily angered, and keeps no record of wrongs; which does not delight in evil but rejoices with the truth; which always protects, trusts, hopes and perseveres (13:4–7).

### The church in Rome: Acts 28:11–31

Paul's arrival at the church in Rome, the capital city of the Empire, forms an appropriate finale, both to the book of Acts and to the apostle's recorded ministry. The letter to the Romans, written some years earlier, concludes with a remarkable series of personal greetings addressed to many of the believers in the Roman community. The list covers twenty-six names in total, quite the most extensive in Paul's correspondence.

Again we are struck by the diversities reflected here. The sheer human breadth of the appeal of Jesus Christ, which we celebrate today in global terms, is certainly no isolated third-millennium reality. As Edward Norman noted years ago, 'There is no need of the human heart that Jesus Christ cannot meet, and that is why Jesus belongs to east and to west, and why no greater than Jesus will ever come. No other is required'.[33] So, too, in first-century Rome, he cast his benign spell over all kinds and conditions of people.

As to race, that there are Jews and Gentiles present is clear from the body of the letter. Major sections are devoted to the issues raised for each by the coming of Jesus Christ. In the final chapter Priscilla and Aquila appear (16:3) as representatives of Jewish Christians, and the list contains many Gentile names. Notable among the latter is Rufus (verse 13), who 'may well have been the son of Simon of Cyrene, who carried Jesus' cross to Golgotha'.[34]

The social-status diversities are also marked. Names such as Ampliatus (verse 8), Urbanus (verse 9), Hermes (verse 14), Philologus and Julia (verse 15) were common slave names. At the other end of the social scale, Aristobulus (verse 10) is probably the grandson of Herod and the friend of Emperor Claudius, and Narcissus (verse 11) is possibly to be identified with the rich and powerful freedman of that name who was an influential advisor to the emperor. Cranfield thinks this identification 'quite probable'.[35]

Finally, we can note the unmistakable gender diversity in the Romans' Christian community. No fewer than nine of the twenty-six names listed are those of women, showing clearly 'that (Paul) was not at all the male chauvinist of popular fantasy'.[36]

There is the hint in chapter 16, particularly at verse 5 ('the church that meets at their house'), that the letter to the Romans may have been addressed to a group of scattered house churches (cf. also verses 10, 11, 14, 15). This is an entirely conceivable circumstance in the densely populated Rome area, bearing in mind that there was no other kind of church in the first century; distinct buildings were a later development within the Rome area. Further, there was no available public-transport system to convey people to a central meeting place, and, additionally, Sunday was not a day of rest within the Empire. If this is in fact the context, the thrust of the letter can then be seen as a sustained plea for the preservation of their unity, particularly in worship.[37]

### With one heart and mouth

Thus 15:6, 'so that with one heart and mouth you may glorify the God and Father of our Lord Jesus Christ', is to be viewed as a primary goal of the entire letter. There is also the call in chapter 14 for the mutual tolerance of 'the strong' and 'the weak' in the case of scruples to do with food laws and ritual observances, another threat to the new-humanity communion. What is certainly clear is that the many diversities reflected among the recipients of the letter – race, rank, religious tradition and gender can all be illustrated – in no way led to their pursuing diverse communal identities.

> We know that they met in houses or household churches ... How was membership of these determined? We cannot suppose that they met according to sex or rank, so that there were different house churches for men and women, for slaves and free. What about race, however? It would be understandable if Jewish Christian and Gentile Christians ... wanted to meet with their own people, because customs and culture are a strong cement to fellowship. But did they? I think not. The toleration of ethnic division in the Roman house churches would be entirely incompatible with Paul's sustained argument for unity in chapters 14 – 15.[38]

*So . . .*

This brief glance at these five first-generation congregations underpins the exegetical conclusions reached in these first two chapters of the book. The new humanity represented a new quality of human community amid the multiple layers and networks of human connectedness that marked the Greco-Roman world. While never perfected, the quality of this new communal life was nonetheless sufficiently distinctive and noteworthy to be a major ground of attraction to the faith that united them.

## The testimony of contemporaries

The social width of these new loyalties is evidenced as Pliny, in the late first century, reports to his emperor concerning 'this contagious superstition', of which 'many of every age, every class, and of both sexes are accused'.[39]

Or we hear Aristides, in the second century, describing Christian lifestyles to the Emperor Hadrian:

> They love one another. They never fail to help widows, they save orphans from those who would hurt them. If they have something they give freely to the man who has nothing; if they see a stranger they take him home, and are happy as though he were a real brother. They don't consider themselves brothers in the usual sense, but brothers instead through the Spirit, in God.[40]

Again, we thrill to the testimony of Justin, writing in the middle of the second century:

> Those who once rejoiced in fornication now delight in continence alone; those who made use of magic arts have dedicated themselves to the good and unbegotten God; we who once took pleasure in the means of increasing our wealth and property now bring what we have into a common fund and share with everyone in need; we who hated and killed one another and would not associate with men of different tribes because of (their different) customs, now after the manifestation of Christ live together and pray for our enemies and try to persuade those who unjustly hate us, so that they, living according to the fair

command of Christ, may share with us the good hope of receiving the same things from God the Master of all.[41]

Or, yet again, Tertullian (155–220) reports that even Christianity's enemies recognized the mutual love of Christians to be their 'distinctive sign': 'Our care for the derelict and our active love have become our distinctive sign before the enemy ... See, they say, how they love one another and how ready they are to die for each other.'[42]

Against the earlier view that the early churches were fairly 'mono-ethnic', David Smith, a former missionary to Nigeria, notes: 'Whereas it was once believed that early Gentile congregations were drawn largely from one level of Graeco–Roman society, closer study of the evidence suggests that, in fact, Christianity broke down social and ethnic barriers and succeeded in holding together a remarkable variety of peoples.'[43]

### The impact

Commentators line up in acknowledgment of the significance of this unique communal lifestyle. 'The impact that the early church made on non-Christians because of Christian brotherhood across natural barriers can hardly be over-estimated,' writes Padilla. 'The abolition of the old separation between Jew and Gentile was undoubtedly one of the most amazing accomplishments of the gospel in the first century. Equally amazing, however, was the breaking down of the class distinction between master and slave.'[44] Michael Green comments, 'When the Christian missionaries not only proclaimed that in Christ the distinctions between slave and free man were done away with as surely as those between Jew and Greek, but actually lived in accordance with their principles, this had an enormous appeal.'[45]

Thus the evidence drawn from the life of the earliest churches confirms the impression gained from a study of the didactic sections of the New Testament letters. The first Christian generations gave expression to their faith in local congregations where diversity in unity was a consistent and celebrated reality. The new humanity which emerged through the New Testament period evinced a new, inclusive form of human society, an all-embracing love, in which the old polarities – Jew/Gentile, male/female, slave/free, elder/youth, powerful/powerless, rich/poor, cultured/uncultured – came under increasing pressure; and precisely here lay a large part of its manifest attractiveness.

# 3  Underpinnings

*Doctrinal confirmations*

The new humanity in Christ through the Holy Spirit is the fundamental form of Christian relating in the New Testament. It is the ideal
that is unapologetically expounded by the apostles in their writings,
and it is the lifestyle that emerged in the fledgling Christian congregations in the book of Acts and that continued on into the following
centuries. Thus the loving, inclusive lifestyle modelled for all time by
Jesus himself was authentically fleshed out by his followers in the
succeeding years.

Our challenge is to relate these biblical realities to the world
of today. Before attempting this we need to face a possible objection.
'All right,' says reader 'John', 'the cumulative case you have made
biblically for the new-humanity congregation is powerful, perhaps
even unanswerable. But how does this conclusion gel with Christian
tradition, like the things I say in my church every Sunday when I recite
the Apostles Creed?' [1]

It is worth taking time to answer this question because it allows us to
strengthen our case even further by exploring ways in which this new-
humanity, unity-in-diversity, together-under-Christ model receives
significant support from primary Christian beliefs. There are at least
six points at which theology buttresses the exegetical conclusions

reached in the first two chapters. The new-humanity congregational model is

- what God is like – the mystery of the Trinity
- what we were made like – the form of creation
- what God became – the wonder of the incarnation
- what God did – the achievement of the atonement
- what the church is called to be – the image of the body
- what we are destined for – the community of glory

### It's what God is like – the mystery of the Trinity

The first underpinning could not be more impressive – the inner life of God himself. Here we tread on holy ground. The inner nature of the Godhead is self-evidently among the 'secret things' which 'belong to the LORD our God' (Deut. 29:29). Indeed, were God himself not to give us *some* access to his inner nature, we would be reduced to silent agnosticism. Here our dependence is total. Only if God speaks of himself can we have reliable knowledge of him. More particularly, only if the God we meet in Jesus Christ through the Scriptures is in some degree an authentic revelation of God in his inner essence can our faith achieve authentic meaning.

To our great relief and joy, in his great mercy he *does* so speak; he *has* so come. In his infinite grace, as Calvin puts it, 'he has descended far beneath his loftiness', and, using the words of the Bible, 'as nurses commonly do with infants, God is wont in a measure to "lisp" to us'.[2]

#### 'God in three persons, blessed Trinity!'

Thus when we ask, 'Who is God?', we are able to answer in the light of Scripture: 'He is One and indivisible, yet existing in three distinguishable persons, God the Father, God the Son, and God the Holy Spirit' (cf. Matt. 3:16–17; 28:19; John 14:15–23; Acts 2:32–36; Rom. 11:36; 2 Cor. 13:14; Eph. 1:3–14; 3:16–19). He is a triune God, three in one, and one in three.

Nearly all the words used in the last two sentences are less than fully adequate for their task. Augustine captured the difficulty at this point when he observed: 'When the question is asked: three *what*?

human language labours altogether under great poverty of speech. The answer, however, is given: three persons, not so that it might be spoken but that it might not be left unspoken.'[3]

But what does this mean? It means that God is diversity in unity. Here is *unity*, each person sharing completely in the divine nature, yet also *diversity*, as each nonetheless evinces points of difference and distinctiveness. What these distinctions are we may indicate only in tentative and general terms.

Thus the Father may be referred to as 'the fount of Deity', yet never in such a way as to imply that the Son and Spirit are less than co-eternal with the Father, existing out of their own everlasting Godhead. The Son may be referred to as 'the Son sent forth by the Father', yet never in such a way as to imply that he does not at all times and at all points repose upon and find his life in and with the Father, and enjoy full deity along with the Father. The Spirit may be viewed as the 'bond of union' between Father and Son, yet never in such a way as to diminish the Spirit's true Godhead, or the equal deity in endless love of all three. Yet they are one Godhead inseparably united. God is Unity in Diversity, Diversity in Unity.

These rather formal distinctions and affirmations come alive for us when we consider the church, because the basic form of the new-humanity church that we have met in the New Testament, as the final goal as well as the provisional, present form of the community of faith, finds reflection in the inner nature of the Godhead.

> The triune God desires that human beings be brought together into a corporate whole, a fellowship of reconciliation which not only reflects God's own eternal reality, but actually participates in that reality. As the church of Jesus Christ ... we are called to pioneer in the present the community of love and thereby to participate in and reflect the eternal revelation of the triune God.[4]

Two things follow. First, this should not surprise us. God is inherently a creative being who delights to express and reflect himself, as the material universe and its endlessly varied life forms bear eloquent witness. Hence it is surely to be expected that his *re*-creative activity, in the outworking of his redemptive purpose, should similarly reflect his nature.

*What an incentive!*

Second, and more important, the diversity-in-unity model could hardly have a greater confirmation than this. For, as we commit ourselves to one another in our churches, and give expression there to a unity of life through the Holy Spirit which affirms and transcends our many differences and diversities, we are actually being God-like! We are following the inner constraint of God the Spirit to reproduce himself, and his likeness, in his human creatures, the special objects of his love and concern.

There can be few greater incentives to work for such diversity-in-unity church communities than this, or greater incentives to keep working at producing them no matter how formidable the obstacles to such unity may appear to be. For in this effort we are actually moving, not just under the impulse of some personal instinct for harmony, but also with the current of the eternal purpose of God which underlies the very universe, and all possible universes, in time and to eternity.

If this theological argument is valid, the plea that lies at the heart of these chapters is a very long way from some personal whim on my part, or a personal desire to promote a particular form of ecclesiastical order for whatever good or dubious reason. We are here carried beyond all such trivia, into the presence of God, the one God, Father, Son and Spirit, who was, and is, and ever will be, to whom be all glory for ever and ever. In his presence we bow in acknowledgment of our endless folly and grossly flawed motivations; but nonetheless here, by grace, we may dare to discern again his call to be like himself, Holy as he is Holy, Love as he is Love, and hence to advocate a form of community among his people that will at least begin, in some degree, to reflect his ever-blessed likeness.[5]

## It's what we were made like – the form of creation

God, as we have just reminded ourselves, is a triune being: Father, Son, Spirit, one God. He is also, and because of this, a creative being. God's nature is necessarily expressed in all his acts of creation, for creation is a form of self-revelation (Ps. 19:1–2; Rom. 1:20). However, as Genesis 1 makes clear, there is a point in his creative work where God discloses himself to a special degree – in the creation of humanity. 'Then God said, "Let us make humans in our image, in our likeness" ... So God created human beings in his own image, in the image of God he created them; male and female he created them' (Gen. 1:26–27).

Hence, human beings, men and women, boys and girls, are in a unique sense reflectors of the nature of God, since they alone are said to express his 'image'. Much ink has been spilled in trying to clarify the exact meaning of 'image' in these verses. One attractive interpretation sees our being God's image-bearers as a call to be the visible, tangible representatives of the transcendent (and hence invisible) Creator.[6]

But in precisely what respects do we 'represent God'? Many recent writers have drawn attention to the words of Genesis 1:27: 'in the image of God ... male and female'. Thus the life of Adam and Eve as a life in mutual relationship takes us to the heart of God's image. So when we read in Genesis 2:24 that 'they will become one flesh', words which clearly were crucial for Jesus in his understanding of human sexuality (cf. Matt. 19:4–6), we see, surely not surprisingly, a reflection of the triune nature of God, hinted at in Genesis 1 and filled out, as we noted above, in the rest of Scripture.[7]

Thus the God who is triune, diversity in unity, creates in his image a being whose essence is also diversity in unity. 'The three members of the Trinity are "person" precisely because they are persons-in-relationship; that is, their personal identities emerge out of their reciprocal relation ... [hence] the Creator's will that humans be the representation of the divine reality means that the goal of human existence is to be persons-in-community.'[8]

### Going home

Thus the form of congregational life in the churches for which we are pleading has a further major undergirding at this point. The model of a diversity realized in unique, divinely mediated community is in fact a *repossession* of the fundamental, God-given form of humanity that was experienced by our first parents before the fall.

Accordingly, to experience this relational aspect of Christian salvation, as for example that believing company at Pentecost did, was actually to be taken back to the Garden of Eden; it was to be afforded even the briefest of tastes of the joys and delights of living together in the very presence of God. So Luke's account artlessly combines these two dimensions: 'Everyone was filled with awe, and many wonders and miraculous signs were done by the apostles. All the believers were together and had everything in common ... Every day they continued to meet together ... they broke bread in their homes and ate together with glad and sincere hearts, praising God, and enjoying the favour of all the people' (Acts 2:43–47). Just for a moment they were visiting Paradise. The new humanity is also the old humanity restored.

When this kind of community begins to be realized in a congregation, one of the things it does is to awaken our primal longings, as people recognize, in some intuitive way, that this is the kind of life for which they were made.

When we were allowed even a small realization of this in our years in Vancouver I lost count of the times people who came into our church for the first time expressed their reaction: 'I somehow felt I had come home.' Precisely ... for we all were there in a sense with Adam and Eve in the Garden, and tasted its joys and fulfilments; we all sinned in their sorry act of folly; we all have been expelled from the Garden of God's intimate presence; we all have lived our lives in the 'far country' of our rebellion against our loving Father. But when, by his gracious initiative, he comes into our far country in the person of his own dear Son, and there meets and embraces us; and, having paid the awful price for our return, turns our steps back again, it is, finally, a joyous homecoming; it is being 'back in the family'; it is 'feeling somehow that I have come home'.

### Science's witness

In our own time this rooting of community in God's original creative intent has found another support, in its own way quite a striking one. For today we are being forced to recognize that reality itself is communal. Community is good science, written into the very texture of the objective world around us. We can illustrate this from two areas: biology and physics.

Biology today works with a very different view of its field than that which operated a few generations ago. Then the model was of an endless round of lethal conflict, 'nature red in tooth and claw'. For social Darwinists, human relations were a matter of the survival of the fittest, overlaid by a thin veneer of civilizing influences. Today biological reality is viewed 'less as a picture of nature focused on the terrors of combat than on the dance of communal collaboration, a picture of the great web of being'.[9]

In physics, the old day of fragmentation, expressed in a concentration on the atom, with a view to reducing reality to smaller and smaller autonomous constituents, has been replaced by a recognition of the importance of integration. Numerous experiments have shown that subatomic particles behave 'as if there were some communication between them'.[10] Thus physicist Henry Stapp can assert: 'An elementary particle is not an independently existing, unanalyzable entity. It is, in essence, a set of relationships that reach outwards to other things.'[11]

Hence the world that has come from the hand of an internally 'diversity-in-unity' Creator exhibits, not surprisingly, multiple marks of interactive and internal relationship; reality is communal.

From this perspective we turn with new comprehension to the so-called 'nature psalms', and worship, with the psalmist, a God concerning whom, in this sense also, 'the heavens declare' his glory, and 'the skies proclaim the work of his hands' (Ps. 19:1). From this perspective also we can celebrate with the prophet the fact that, not just at the fullness of the messianic kingdom but even now, 'the mountains and hills will burst into song before you, and all the trees of the field will clap their hands' (Isa. 55:12).

Small wonder, then, that such a God invites his 'new creation' to imitate his old creation by calling for 'community' to be again the determinative reality of our lives.

## It's what God became – the wonder of the incarnation

It is impossible to overstate the crucial place of Christology, the doctrine of Christ, in any responsible account of the Christian faith. All the lines and trajectories of Christian theology pass through this central point, and that applies as much to our understanding of the church and its mission as to anything else.

In the person of Jesus there is a unique union of Godhood and humanity. Here the diversity expressed in the eternal, irreducible distinction between Creator and creature is transcended in the mystery and miracle of incarnation; 'the Word became flesh and made his dwelling among us' (John 1:14).

### 'Our God contracted to a span'

The sheer wonder and awesomeness of the incarnation is best approached in the company of the kneeling shepherds and wise men; best expressed in the poetic word:

> Blue homespun and the bend of my breast
> keep warm this small hot naked star
> fallen into my arms...
> Quiet he lies
> whose vigour hurled a universe. He sleeps
> whose eyelids have not closed before.
> His breath (so slight it seems
> no breath at all) once ruffled the dark deeps
> to sprout a world...
> Breath, mouth, ears, eyes
> he is curtailed who overflowed all skies,
> all years. Older than eternity, now he
> is new...
> (Luci Shaw)[12]

The fullness of deity, and the fullness of humanity, became one in the person of the Mediator, Jesus Christ. How does this connect with our unity-in-diversity, new-humanity fellowship in the Holy Spirit?

### Embracing the other

Firstly, it mandates the propriety of that 'embrace of the other' which lies at the heart of unity in diversity. In the incarnation, God the Creator takes into authentic unity with himself that which is not himself, namely, his creature. In respect of all possible ranges of difference between beings, the gulf that was crossed in the incarnation was the widest conceivable. The eternal became one with the temporal, the infinite with the finite, the uncreated with the created, the transcendent with the immanent, the divine with the human, the holy with the vulnerable and temptable; truly, as C. S. Lewis recognized, 'the grand miracle'.[13] No wonder the adoring songs of heaven came bursting through the curtain of sense at such a deed (Luke 2:13–14).

In the light of the incarnation, the 'embrace of the other' within the community of the church is afforded supreme authentication. To respond to the call to love, in the name of the divine love, one who is different from myself, is seen as a fundamentally good and proper thing. It is finally a divine thing. It is a call to walk where God walked in his taking up, in embracing as his own, our very humanity. Here too, in his 'work' of incarnation as in his work of creation, 'God saw all that he had made, and it was very good' (Gen. 1:31). Here, too, even for us in *our* embrace of the other, that 'very good' may be uttered.

Secondly, the incarnation establishes the possibility of transcending difference. The fact that the supreme gulf of being which stretches between the Creator and the creature was overcome in the person of Jesus Christ implies that every lesser gulf, specifically that which stretches between two human beings, is in principle bridgeable, for the God who indwells us is the God who defines himself as the great 'gulf-crosser' or 'reconciler' (Rom. 5:10–11; 2 Cor. 5:18–20; Eph. 2:16; Col. 1:20).

The unifying possibilities that emerge when this God of incarnation comes himself into our lives and congregations by his Holy Spirit are accordingly unlimited. While we are never perfected on this side of the kingdom's full arrival, the many references to the Spirit's ministry of outpoured love are impressive (cf. 1 Cor. 12 – 14, including chapter 13 in particular; Rom. 5:5; 14:17; 2 Cor. 13:10; Gal. 5:22–23; Eph. 4:3; 5:19–20; 1 Thess. 4:9).

In the face of our instinctive, human fear of the other, the incarnation brings hope and promise. And we require these things, for, let us be honest, all relationships with our human neighbours involve a degree of risk, even threat. Relationship requires that we admit within the boundaries of our selfhood the other, who is neither entirely accessible to our understanding nor entirely submitted to our control. The greater the distance the neighbour is from our regular sphere of understanding and experience, the greater the risk and threat involved in the relationship. This is why, as sociologists demonstrate, we are more comfortable with 'people like us' (see also chapter 9 below).

If, of course, we are dealing in Christian missiology only with human factors, then the theory is difficult to challenge. But, in the new humanity in Christ, we are not determined by the merely human. If we are, then we have ceased to be the church in any authentically biblical sense. In the love-gift of the Holy Spirit, which is the sole base of Christian belonging and community, we can experience a reality that overcomes the fear-driven antipathies of our natural instincts, through identifying the indwelling Spirit in the neighbour with the same indwelling Spirit in our own hearts.

Thus the neighbour, no matter how different, becomes a sister or a brother, to whom, and with whom, we belong eternally in one body. In Jesus' timeless parable of the good Samaritan, the different neighbour, whom we fear even when met in a broken, helpless state lying by a roadside, becomes the object of our loving embrace and self-sacrificing concern. The fear-ridden priest, too, may become, by the Spirit, the good Samaritan. This miracle of grace, which is one of the sweetest fruits of Calvary, lies at the heart of the new humanity, and finds its ultimate authorization in the 'Word made flesh', in the God who is Emmanuel, 'God with us'.

### 'That they may be one'

Finally, the incarnation additionally affords us the prayer of Jesus, the incarnate one, for the unity of his people (John 17:11, 20–23), a unity of the same quality as that existing between the persons of the Trinity. 'My prayer is . . . that all of them may be one, Father, just as you are in me and I am in you . . . that they may be one as we are one; I in them and you in me. May they be brought to complete unity to let the world know that you sent me' (John 17:20–23).

As our enthroned High Priest, clothed still in his humanity, he intercedes in the heavens (Rom. 8:34; Heb. 7:25) as he awaits the fulfilment of his prayer in this present age and in the age to come. If *our* feeble prayers, including those for unity, can be guaranteed an answer when offered 'in Jesus' name' (John 16:24), how much more is that guarantee attached to Jesus' prayers offered in Jesus' name!

Incarnation means the utter propriety of, and eternal hopefulness for, authentic diversity in unity.

### It's what God did – the achievement of the atonement

The union of divine and human in the incarnation, the supreme model of embrace of the different other, is not a stopping point. Incarnation in itself, for all its glorious achievement, cannot realize the ultimate purpose of the love of God – namely, to embrace the human other in an enduring communion. 'It is not in [Christ's] being here, but in his being here as a propitiation for the sins of the world, that the love of God is revealed ... Not Bethlehem but Calvary is the focus of revelation.'[14]

If that final goal of God's love is to be achieved, two further requirements must be met. First, the implications of the sinful rebellion of the human partner need to be confronted and over-come in a manner consistent with God's loving and holy nature; and second, the human partners need to experience an internal transformation which separates them from the continuing, fallen inclination to rebel against God, and, consequently, also against their human neighbours.

## No bypassing the cross

It needs to be noted, further, that both of these requirements make sense, and derive their theological and moral necessity, on the basis of a quite specific biblical perspective, by which an almighty, infinite, eternal God creates a universe that reflects his nature.

Accordingly, this is, firstly, a *relational* universe, because God is himself relational in the mutual love of the three persons of the Godhead; and secondly, this is a *moral* universe, because God is holy (Lev. 11:44; 19:2; Josh. 24:19; 1 Sam. 6:20; Ps. 16:10; 22:3; Isa. 57:15; John 17:11; Acts 2:27; 1 Thess. 4:8; 1 Pet. 1:16; 1 John 1:5; Rev. 4:8).

This means, reflecting the root meaning of the word 'holy', that the Triune, personal God separates himself from all that contradicts who he is: from unlove, because he is love; from falsehood, because he is truth; from disloyalty, because he is faithful; from despising and abusing other people, because he loves and cares for them; from the worship of other gods, because he alone is God; from evil, because he is good; from sin, because he is righteous.

In sum, God has made a universe of moral order within which, as his creatures, we are called upon to live lives that joyfully reflect God and accord with his nature as holy love. Such is our dignity as moral beings.

It is this biblical revelation of the moral order of the universe that enables us to understand, in turn, four realities: the fact of our sin and its seriousness, God's wrath with respect to it, our entire inability to save ourselves, and the reason why God can pardon and reconcile us to himself and to each other only by bearing the consequences of our sin himself.

All of that came together in the inexhaustible glory of God's atoning deed at the cross. As we saw in chapter 1, when examining Ephesians 2:13–18, 'through the blood of Christ' (2:13) the hostility was slain, and peace was made, both vertically between humanity and God, and horizontally between human neighbour and human neighbour.

> I hear the words of love
> I gaze upon the blood,
> I see the mighty sacrifice,
> And I have peace with God.
> (Horatius Bonar)

But not only peace with God; peace also with the fellow members of his family; for, as was established in our earlier discussion, God's amazing deed of love in sacrificing himself in the person of Christ for his creatures' sins mandates a Christian community in which all who are reconciled to God are automatically also reconciled to each other in a new humanity. Here the goal of embracing the different neighbour was normatively realized and authenticated.

But, as Paul Pearce argues, another remarkable incentive for working to produce new-humanity, diversity-in-unity, 'together-under-Christ' congregations is established by this linkage to the atone-ment: 'Ephesians 2:15b–16 provides the foundational statement for the formation of Christian community, and the rest of the letter is the blueprint of the church. To not work toward the model of unity and community outlined throughout the rest of the New Testament would be a denial of the reason for Christ's sacrificial work on the cross.'[15]

Putting this point positively, the forming of such churches honours Christ's sacrifice. It brings glory to our blessed Lord by enabling the spoils of his terrible and yet glorious victory to become evident. Thus, from this perspective, it is a means of enabling our Lord Jesus to 'see the result of the suffering of his soul and be satisfied' (Isa. 53:11, NIV footnote). 'Lift high the cross!' we cry, and rightly so. And here is how to do it: build congregations of reconciliation.

## It's what the church is called to be – the image of the body

The primary New Testament image for the church is the body of Christ (cf. Rom. 12:5; 1 Cor. 10:16; 12:12–30; Eph. 4:12; 5:23; Col. 1:18; 2:19). It is a Pauline image the importance of which is widely acknowledged. 'The Pauline concept of the Body of Christ forcefully suggests itself as the most mature result of New Testament thinking about the church.'[16]

At the core of this image is the conviction that Christians have been re-created into a new existence in which they become participants in the continuing life of the risen Jesus Christ; Christians are 'one body with Christ' (cf. Rom. 12:5). The source of the image was surely Paul's life-changing meeting with the risen Lord outside Damascus. There his astonished question, 'Who are you, Lord?', receives the answer, 'I am Jesus, whom you are persecuting' (Acts 9:5). 'The appearance on which Paul's whole faith and apostleship was founded was the revelation of the resurrection body of Christ, not as an individual, but as the Christian community.' Thus 'from the day he saw Christ in the church he was persecuting, it seems he can no longer look into the eyes of a Christian without meeting there the gaze of Christ'.[17]

It is this 'horizontal' dimension, our relationships with one another in the one body of Christ, that Paul explores when struggling with the lack of mutual unity within the churches he addresses, particularly so at Corinth (1 Cor. 12:12–30) and Rome (Rom. 12:3–8), and he turns to it again in Ephesians when expounding God's purpose for the church (4:7–12).

The biblical understanding of the church as conveyed in this primary New Testament image is of a community where rich, God-given diversity is brought into a supernaturally formed communion of life; the life of a new humanity.

### Many members, one body

In the primary passages in which we encounter this image, there is clear stress also on the massive diversity that is the starting point. So Romans 12:4–5 says: 'Just as each of us has one body with *many* members, and these members do not all have the same function, so in Christ we who are *many* form one body, and each member belongs to all the others' (my italics). Or in 1 Corinthians 12:12–14 we read: 'The body is a unit, though it is made up of *many* parts; and though all its parts are *many*, they form one body. So it is with Christ ... Now the body is not made up of one part but of *many*' (my italics). The diversity is further underlined in the subsequent 'member' examples: the foot and the hand, the ear and the eye (verses 14–17). Clearly, the assumption is of a significant heterogeneity in these congregations, as the raw material from which is constituted the humanly inexplicable unity with which they are to learn to function.

### Start local

This 'body' model is primarily expressed in the local Christian congregation. The local church dominates the scene in the New Testament. True, the vision of God's *cosmic* purpose for his people is always in the background. But the local congregation is where that vision is to be worked out and given hands and feet. So the apostolic letters are mainly addressed to local groups of Christians gathered in specific locations.

Further, when the story of the early church is told by Luke in the book of Acts, we are introduced again and again to the founding of local churches as representing the bridgehead for the progress and expansion of the faith. The story of the expansion of the church universal is the story of the founding and effective function of the church local.

T. M. Lindsay, in his widely respected exposition of the church and its ministry, noted that biblical usage knows virtually nothing of the primary word for the church, *ekklēsia*, being used to refer to the universal company of Christ's followers.

> It must be admitted that the *word* 'church' is seldom used in the New Testament to designate one, universal and comprehensive society. On the contrary, out of the 110 times in which the word occurs, no less than 100 do not contain this note of a wide-spreading unity. In the overwhelming majority of cases the word 'church' denotes a local Christian society, varying in extent from all the Christian congregations within a province of the Empire to a small assembly of Christians meeting together in the house of one of the brethren.[18]

This is widely recognized today. 'The basic form of Christian witness is a company of the followers of Jesus called by God's Spirit and joined together as God's people in a particular place ... the concrete life of the particular community is the essential expression of our rootedness in the particularism of Judaism and Jesus.'[19]

### The body of Christ

Applied in this local context the body-of-Christ image powerfully expresses the heart of the new humanity. Here is the *diversity* represented by the divers limbs and organs of the body. Here is the transcending *unity*, the body's one life system that gathers all the particular parts into a single whole. And here is the Head, the risen, reigning Christ, the vivifying centre, because of whose presence the congregation can only be understood as a supernatural reality, defying the reductionist analysis of a secular society, created and maintained by the Lord and his almighty Spirit.

All this does not imply that larger expressions of unity are irrelevant to the new-humanity vision (see chapter 6). However, at this point again, theological confession – 'I believe in ... the holy catholic church' – meshes tidily with, and undergirds, the new-humanity vision we have developed.

## It's what we are destined for – the community of glory

Our first point of theological justification took us to the very beginning of the Bible. Our final justification takes us to the other end of the Bible's temporal spectrum, the climax of history in the last book of Scripture, Revelation.

There, humanity recovers the Garden from which it was driven by sin (cf. Gen. 2:8–15; 3:1–24; Rev. 22:1–2). There Creator and creature renew their interrupted communion (Gen. 1:27–31; Rev. 21:3; 22:3–5). There God's human viceroys, the ones made to reign and have dominion under God's supreme authority, stand tall again, fulfilling once more God's purpose as his regents, ruling his renewed earth (Gen. 1:26–31; Ps. 8:5–6; Heb. 2:7–8; Rev. 22:5).

### For ever ... together with the Lord

The vision of the end, however, is consistently corporate. Whether the Bible depicts the final order as a perfect city (Rev. 21:2), a victorious kingdom (Heb. 12:28), a holy temple (Ezek. 40 – 48) or a wedding feast (Rev. 19:7), the images all reflect a perfected human society where God's people live together in endless love and mutual service (Rev. 22:3). The final vision in Revelation makes reference to 'his people' (21:3), living together in a resplendent city (21:2, 22–23). It speaks of 'the nations' walking by its light (21:24), and the dimensions of the city, necessarily symbolic as they no doubt are, nonetheless conveying a picture of massive size – 'staggeringly large', to cite one New Testament scholar.[20]

A closer look at this supremely privileged company is afforded in Revelation 7:9–17. Following the three-layered, cyclical form of the developing visions of Revelation, this passage occurs towards the end of the first cycle, covering the sweep of human history under the image of the seven opened seals (Rev. 5:1–5; 6:1 – 8:5). The passage gives us a fore-vision of the whole company of the ransomed people of God at the climax of history as the seventh seal is opened, and the end, sprung finally by the prayers of the saints across the ages (8:3–4), is realized in apocalyptic judgment (8:5) and redemption.

*Who are they?*
So who are these ransomed people? John tells us:

> I looked and there before me was a great multitude that no-one could count, from every nation, tribe, people and language, standing before the throne and in front of the Lamb. They were wearing white robes and were holding palm branches in their hands. And they cried out in a loud voice:

> > 'Salvation belongs to our God,
> > who sits on the throne,
> > and to the Lamb.'
> (Rev. 7:9–10)

Jesus had spoken of this global company in terms of their geographical points of origin: 'I say to you many will come from the east and the west, and will take their places at the feast with Abraham, Isaac and Jacob in the kingdom of heaven' (Matt. 8:11). He spoke, too, of his 'other sheep that are not of this sheep pen. I must bring them also. They too will listen to my voice, and there shall be one flock and one shepherd' (John 10:16); for 'I, when I am lifted up from the earth, will draw all people to myself' (John 12:32; cf. 11:52).

Behind this again is the Old Testament promise to Abraham that through him and his offspring 'all peoples on earth will be blessed' (Gen. 12:3). Accordingly, as the Messiah who will effect this universal redemption is anticipated within the community of Israel (Abraham's offspring), he is proclaimed as 'a light for the Gentiles, that you may bring my salvation to the ends of the earth' (Isa. 49:6; cf. 42:6).

### All nations and peoples of every language

The clearest anticipation of Revelation 7:9–17, however, occurs, not surprisingly, in its Old Testament counterpart, the book of Daniel. There we are given the equivalent fore-vision of history's climax before the throne of final judgment (Dan. 7:9–12). There, too, we meet the 'Son of Man', the personal instrument of the judgments and salvation of God (7:13–14). There, too, are his people: 'all nations and peoples of every language worshipped him. His dominion is an everlasting dominion that will not pass away, and his kingdom is one that will never be destroyed' (7:14).

Appropriately, the focus of the vision is on the Son of Man himself; the people are part of the train that surrounds him, and their service enhances the triumph and glory of his reign. That emphasis is in the deepest sense correct; we ever exist for him and his praise. However, we are not forbidden a glance at his company. Whether through the eyes of Daniel in the old covenant (= testament), or John in the new, we are inevitably struck by their all-inclusive diversity. 'All nations and peoples of every language', declares Daniel; 'a great multitude that no-one could count, from every nation, tribe, people and language', cries John.

### Beyond the United Nations

Here is diversity as it has never been experienced during the entirety of history. No United Nations mandate has ever summoned such a heterogeneous company. Nor will it, no matter how long history plays out, for this company includes, as Jesus noted in Matthew 8:11, not only the geographical breadth of human community, representing every nation on earth's face, but also the succession of the generations across history's passing ages.

It is into this astonishing, unprecedented, multi-coloured, multi-generational, multi-racial, multi-everything community that we are headed if we belong to Jesus Christ, the saving Son of Man. This all-inclusive community will be our human family and people of identity into the ages of eternity.

Indeed, beside them and the duration of our belonging among them, our identities and relationships here pale into an insignificant temporariness. My Scottishness, or Canadianness, or Africanness, or Americanness, or Mexicanness, or Chineseness, or whatever our present ethnic or racial identity may be, will all be left behind – not in the sense that we will lose the richness of our national and cultural inheritance, for 'the glory and honour of the nations will be brought into it [the city]' (Rev. 21:26). But our sense of belonging, the final anchorage of our identity, will expand to embrace this amazingly diverse and yet wonderfully united company, the followers of the Lamb, the blood-bought family of the Lord.

### Glory begun below

Since that is our destined future, does this not powerfully imply that it is to such new humanity, diversity in unity, that we should bend our hearts and reach our loyalties in the present? Does this not call for the creation of Christian communities in our local churches that express God's multi-coloured, multi-everything diversity of today and anticipate God's multi-coloured, multi-everything diversity of tomorrow – churches that accordingly bring heaven to earth?

To embrace our 'different' neighbours will be among the culminating delights of our coming salvation. But we can get onto that trajectory into God's future *this very day*, as we reach out here and now across all the barriers of diversity, to embrace those 'different' neighbours who belong with us in Jesus Christ.

### Tomorrow, today

Thus, if we are Christians, the diversity-in-unity, new-humanity church, whether we are attracted to it or not, just happens to be our future, on the day when we shall, at last, love the Lord our God with all our heart and soul and mind and strength, and our neighbours as ourselves (Mark 12:30–31).

Experiencing even something of that reality here and now is, therefore, as the old hymn expresses it, quite literally 'glory begun below'. New-humanity community is a love-gift of the Holy Spirit, who, as the life of heaven experienced on earth (Rom. 8:23; 2 Cor. 1:22; Eph. 1:14), encourages us in our pursuit of it here, and is the promise of our participation in it there. Such 'diversity-in-unity' congregational life is supremely fulfilling, and the joys of it need not await our death or the Lord's coming. We can begin to taste its blessings now, in our local church, next Sunday!

Hence the triune nature of God, his creation of humanity and the world, the person and atoning work of Jesus Christ, the form of the church, and the future life of the kingdom, all combine in one grand conclusion: the diversity-in-unity model which we identified in the Scriptures (chapters 1 and 2) receives massive endorsement from the great doctrines that are explored in this chapter.

## 4  An idea whose hour has come

*Into the world of today*

What should churches look like as they gather for worship? As we drop by the local church on the next corner, what might we hope to see? The conviction that drives this book is that churches should strike us with their obvious diversity; an evident mix of people warmly committed to one another, as well as to the living Lord, who is at the centre of their life and worship.

Even if the congregation is situated in a mainly homogeneous neighbourhood in respect of ethnic origins, we would hope to see good numbers of both men and women, clearly comfortable together, with all the age groups and generations represented, plus signs of different kinds of family structure, different wealth levels, and probably indications of diversity in regard to how long the individuals or family units have been part of the congregation. Hopefully there might also be signs of a spread of work setting between blue-collar and professional, and evidence of people who are still seeking for a personal Christian faith, as well as the mature, seasoned believers. Here and there the presence of people with physical or mental challenges would indicate a further expression of the congregation's diversity.

Before proceeding to see how all this works out in the 'trenches' of congregational life, we shall in the next two chapters explore a further highly stimulating, experience-based argument in support of this vision. Being experience-based rather than Scripture-based, it is necessarily less weighty, but it is nonetheless persuasive in its own terms. It is the witness of present history. For the fact is that this new-humanity model of the church is massively endorsed by the global realities that surround us every day. If ever there was an idea whose time has come, it is precisely this way of doing church.

In his book *The Cross-Cultural Process in Christian History*, Andrew Walls explores the nature of the new humanity of Ephesians 2:15 and is in accord with our earlier recognition of its epochal status. 'While the anticipation must have been of two distinct Christian communities, Jew and Gentile, the Ephesian letter has not even a dream of such an outcome.'[1] He acknowledges that this 'Ephesian Moment' was 'quite brief' – the destruction of the Jewish state in AD 70, the scattering of the Jewish church and the sheer success of the Gentile mission meant that the church very soon became again monocultural, 'as overwhelmingly Hellenistic as it had been overwhelmingly Jewish'. Nevertheless, Walls concludes, 'in our own day the Ephesian moment has come again, and come in a richer mode than has ever happened since the first century'.[2]

Let us explore the exciting scenario that underlies that claim. We begin by contemplating the modern world and identifying three of its cardinal features.

## A diversifying world

In his worldwide bestseller *Future Shock*, written as long ago as 1970, Alvin Toffler predicted: 'The human race, far from being flattened into monotonous conformity, will become far more diverse socially than it ever was before.'[3]

By the time he followed that up with *The Third Wave*, ten years later, the prediction was already being fulfilled. 'Meanwhile two things cut through everything as the Third Wave thunders in our ears. One is the shift toward a higher level of diversity in society – the de-massification of mass society. The second is acceleration – the faster pace at which historical change occurs. Together these place tremendous strains on individuals and institutions alike, intensifying the super-struggle as it rages about us.'[4]

## Like never before

Today we are facing social diversity in all of our cultures 'as never before' in human history. To quote a chapter heading in Ray Bakke's *The Urban Christian*: 'The Lord is shaking up the world.'[5] Ethnic diversity is the most obvious and visible form of this upheaval. The teeming world cities have become mosaics of national sub-groups.

Driven by massive international migrations, spawned in many cases by wars and ethnic conflicts, hundreds of millions have abandoned their family roots and set out to find new lands in which to live. This has become a commonplace for city-dwellers. Here a Canadian suburban pastor describes the congregation he looks out upon:

> On any given Sunday morning you could witness a struggling-with-ESL [English as a second language] Chinese space-aeronautics engineer, currently selling radios at Future Shop, handing a service bulletin to a recently arrived Español Colombian environmental economics professor who is exiled from his work with Colombia's indigenous. Both will stumble through an English hymn, along with an Iranian pseudo-Muslim telecommunications specialist, who sits beside an unemployed French-Canadian warehouser on one side, and a Japanese exchange student on the other, and in front of a '1.5 generation' Korean teenager and behind the elder Mennonite, a recent widower.

We can put the same reality more formally in terms of statistical numbers. For example, of the approximately 175 distinct nations identified by the United Nations, 135 are significantly represented in my adopted country of Canada. In London, children in the school system speak a staggering 300 different languages. In Miami, foreign-born residents number 59% of the resident population, followed by Toronto with 44%, Los Angeles with 41%, and Vancouver in the global fourth spot with 39%. In Los Angeles the Southern Baptists worship in 52 languages every Sunday. In Amsterdam there are 44 distinct ethnic neighbourhoods. In Birmingham, in the very centre of England, the ethnic-minority population is 30%.

Other criteria of diversification tell the same story. In the sphere of age and generational difference there is a greater spread of distinct generational identities than at any previous time, caused largely by the ageing of many populations. Thus in the United Kingdom in the period spanning 1901 to 1981, while the percentage in the under-14-year-old bracket fell from 32.4% to 20.5%, the percentage over 65 more than trebled, from 4.7% to 15%.

Family structures are also diversifying. In the United States, often a social barometer for Western societies, we can cite a report for the years 1960–90.[6] In the thirty years covered by the data, the percentage of the population living in two-parent families fell from 74% to 54%; the percentage in single-parent families rose from 10% to 17%; and those outside any family structure doubled from 15% to 30% of the total population. In addition, husband–wife households with only one working spouse accounted in 1990 for only 14% of all households, as compared with 43% in 1960. Wives contributed about 43% of the family income in 1990, compared to 25% in 1982.

By 1990, at least thirteen distinct types of household had eclipsed the traditional family, including such categories as 'female head, widowed, with children' and 'male head, previously married, with children'. More than a third of the couples first married in the 1970s had divorced by the mid-1980s; more than a third of the children born in the 1970s spent part of their childhood in single-parent family settings. The years that have passed since these figures were published have certainly not reversed any of these trends.

Every pastor knows very well the relational chaos that reigns in many communities today. The 'pastoral issues' courses taught in seminaries and theological colleges in the 1960s and earlier, which were intended as a preparation for pastoral dilemmas, are largely irrelevant. I computed that in my pastoral work in Vancouver I was faced at times with more of these dilemmas in an average week than my seminary course had covered in a year. Issues over marriage, remarriage and divorce; pregnancies, both unwanted and longed for; HIV/Aids; abortion; homosexuality; addiction; transsexuality; money and employment; implications of conversion from a different faith tradition, involving even potential threats to life; legal issues, such as the custody of children, rights to an estate, and what constitutes sexual abuse or unlawful dismissal – the list goes on and on. Much of this is simply the symptom of massive diversity, creating multiple interfaces in values and lifestyles between the old and the new.

The wider spread of wealth (and again I am focusing primarily on Western societies here) has also encouraged greater diversity as more people have access to more varied opportunities and the significantly enhanced mobility, both social and geographical, that this provides. This has produced a new middle class in many countries, with greater access to wealth, although in the process the wealth gap between the rich and the poor has tragically continued to widen rather than diminish – a matter of serious concern both globally and locally.

Another index of diversity is simply the range of people in touch with churches today. As an example I may cite a not untypical baptismal service, which I particularly recall for the sheer diversity of the thirteen candidates that Sunday morning: a ladies' hairdresser; a First Nations Crow Indian chief and his wife; a physical-education teacher from North Vancouver; a hospital psychiatrist; a former call-girl from the Kitsilano district; a mother and homemaker from Holland; a converted biker from Aberdeen, Scotland; an investment banker from Hong Kong; a doctor from a hospital emergency department; an eleven-year-old school student from Hawaii; a science student from the university; and finally a Hungarian tightrope walker and trapeze artist!

The greater ease and the speed of travel have also contributed, as has the internationalization of business, as well as a global media and communications network, fuelled by the personal computer and the mobile phone.

### 'He wants to become a Christian!'

Let me illustrate where we are today, as far as global communication is concerned, with this delightful story from the Farsi congregation in Toronto recently.

The members of the congregation were happy to welcome a new woman, but were a bit nonplussed by her habit of talking into her cell phone during the sermon on Sunday mornings. The pastor's wife, who always knows, of course, how much goes into the preparation, decided to take the matter in hand, and challenged the woman: of course she was very welcome, but her husband spent so much time faithfully preparing; could she not show more respect?

The visitor explained: 'Oh, no, it's not that I don't respect your husband. During the message I dial up *my* husband in Baghdad, and he listens to it on the phone, and I try and answer his questions as the message goes along; and he is very interested. He's in a secret Bible study of six people and they are all seeking the Lord.'

Well! Of course the visitor was moved to the front pew! And imagine the joy a few weeks later when in the middle of the message the woman cried out, 'He wants to become a Christian!' The pastor broke into his sermon, came down from the pulpit, and over the phone led the husband to Christ in Baghdad; then went back into the pulpit and finished his message, while the congregation were signing hallelujahs in the background!

### It's in your face!
But as well as the increase in 'sheer diversity' – that is, diversity as sociologically identifiable – there is what one might call 'experiential diversity'. This refers to the diversity we experience in our daily life. In some ways, as far as the implications for forming congregations are concerned, this is more significant.

Carol, a nurse in the maternity unit of a local hospital, describes her staff-nurse colleagues: 'It's really a mini-United Nations. We have nurses from Ethiopia, Ireland, Iran, Singapore, Australia, the Philippines, South Africa, India, Canada, Malaysia and the United Kingdom.' She refers to a couple having a baby in the unit, who, to her surprise, were conversing in very simple, basic English, because, as she discovered, that was their only language of communication. The father was from Camanchka in Russia, and the mother from Japan, and they had met at an 'English as a second language' class.

Another couple, Christians, consisted of Hyen, a former Buddhist from Vietnam but brought up in Winnipeg in Central Canada, and Nazim, a former Hindu from India, brought up in Ontario. When Carol asked if they had problems with the cultural diversity in their backgrounds, she was met with a blank stare. 'But we're both Canadians!'

Putting this another way, we inhabit a society today where it is increasingly less possible to escape into ghettos of similarity ('my kind of people'). The increase of wealth and its wider distribution means that neighbourhoods are more stratified; the internationalization of economics, business and professional life, as well as the greatly increased ethnic diversity, particularly in cities, also increases the diversity of life's daily encounters. I can no longer, or am less and less able to, avoid my 'different' neighbour.

## A postmodern world

This trend in human social connections is paralleled by the theoretical axioms of what is generally referred to as postmodernism. While it is much more than a set of propositions, postmodernism is widely seen as riding on the back of a few formal propositions of which none is more significant than the assumption of the imprisoning of each individual within the biases and rationalizations of his or her own self-interests. Accordingly, truth is always only 'my truth' or 'your truth'. The grand optimistic assumption of modernism, stemming from the Enlightenment, regarding the existence of a universal reason and universal meaning, has been abandoned. All that we have, accordingly, is a multiplicity of viewpoints and perspectives. In this contemporary mood the individual becomes supreme, and the diversity of global society and culture becomes the determinative axiom of existence.

Today's is a 'stirred-up' world, with no likelihood of any reversal of the trend. In this third millennium since Jesus Christ walked our earth, diversity has become the stuff of human civilization all over the globe. In such a world the times cry out for a church model that faces this reality directly, and which is able to harness its potential for the kingdom of God.

## A unifying world

Paradoxically, just as the world becomes more complex and diverse, it is experiencing unprecedented trajectories towards unification. This is the reality of globalization. As never before, we live in one world. The symbol for life today is the green ball, Earth as perceived from space, one world. The mood is perceptively caught in a comment by *Discovery 8* astronaut Sultan bin Salman al-Saud: 'The first day or so we all pointed to our countries. The third or fourth day we were pointing to our continents. By the fifth day we were aware of only one earth.'[7] As Howard Snyder perceptively observes, 'For the first time children are coming to adulthood with a global consciousness.'[8]

## Just Earth

The usual way to refer to this change is by the term 'globalization'. The academic community and the public sphere continue to debate the precise meaning and significance of globalization. David Held offers this definition: 'the widening, deepening and speeding up of worldwide interconnectedness in all aspects of contemporary, social life'.[9]

Snyder explores the implications. Noting the distinctions coined in the 1970s and 1980s of the First, Second and Third Worlds, he writes:

> These distinctions are now obsolete. Global economic links, the collapse of communism, and the new information age make these distinctions meaningless, or at least misleading. We are moving from three worlds to one: just Earth. This trend is the base force leading to a new global society by 2030. In science, entertainment, business, or politics, globalization is the shaping force.[10]

No consensus has, of course, been reached on the positive or negative impact of globalization. Anthony Giddens writes: 'We are being propelled into a global order that no one fully understands, but which is making its effect felt upon all of us.'[11]

## Thinking globally

But this newborn sense of global identity is hugely important as far as our mental world is concerned. It inevitably stirs the imagination, not least that of the emerging generations, challenging our merely personal and national ambitions, disturbing our narrow preoccupations and awakening at a certain level our dreams of belonging to a family that transcends the divisive negativism of so much of modern life and connects us to a community of truth, acceptance and beauty, of love, kindness and purity, where we can unite with all our human family and make a difference in our desperately needy world.

One of the paradoxes of the appearance and growth of this global 'skin' is the way in which it has also produced fragmentations, and even a certain type of localization. This is explored by Roland Robertson in a book that coins the somewhat unattractive term 'glocalization'. He notes that globalization always take place, and has an impact, in a specific local setting; and that one of the effects of the global forces is to cause local markets and communities to morph their identity to suit the global forces and in the process become more self-consciously themselves.[12]

This glocalizing effect reminds us that in reviewing our world we need to find a place to recognize both these developments that we have surveyed – diversity in terms of social and communal pluralisms at every level, and unity in terms of overarching forces which transcend national and tribal identities.

### Coming apart and rushing together

Today's reality was perceptively caught by *The Atlantic* magazine: 'The world is coming dangerously apart and rushing precipitously together at the same time'. Sociologist Peter Dray notes the same ambiguity: 'on the one hand increasing complexity as we enter the "network society" where the increasingly extended networks produce increasing complexity'. Yet at the same time, 'globalization is also concerned with the increasing homogenization of cultures and tastes with the standardized products produced by global corporations with no allegiance to place or community'. Hence 'globalization is a tension of two processes in making networks more complex . . . and an overall framework of increasing homogenization of content'.[13]

Thus, unprecedented diversification at every level of human society, and an unprecedented awareness of being bound together in a single, global family, represent the twin reference points that plot our time and place on planet Earth. The combination of these two realities and their myriad, multi-layered interactions constitute the essential human experience in these opening years of the third millennium. What is surely required of us within the sphere of the church at such a time is to find a way of developing our communities of faith that is rooted in the normative, timeless revelation of Scripture, that enables us to face the challenging realities of our time with confidence, and that will facilitate our harnessing their potential for the sake of the kingdom and glory of God.

### A world where Jesus is Lord

We complete this glance at the contemporary world by noting, alongside these two significant features, a third. This one is of a different order. Indeed, whereas the other two are 'in your face' and universally recognized, this third is perceived only from the perspective of faith. Yet it is, in the final analysis, of infinitely greater importance. This is a world where Jesus is Lord.

As we saw in our consideration of Ephesians 1:10, God's purpose to bring all things together under Christ has historic precedent. 'He [God] raised him [Christ] from the dead and seated him at his right hand in the heavenly realms' (Eph. 1:20). For Paul, as for his master, resurrection means reign (cf. Matt. 28:18) – hence Christ's present rule at this moment over all the earth, and here and now right where we are as we read these sentences. Such has been the heart of Christian conviction across all the centuries.

### Risen and reigning

The fact of the resurrection is a fundamental axiom of the Christian theory of knowledge, as Paul was not hesitant to assert to his philosophical audience in Athens (Acts 17:31). James Stewart memorably captures the scene:

> 'When they heard of the Resurrection, some mocked' ... Twenty centuries have echoed the laughter of the Areopagus. But here in the resurrection is the fact which at the first launched Christianity upon the world and conquered the throne of the Caesars; here is the rock upon which the church was built and has stood for two thousand years; here is the good news which, a million times, has dried the tears of the desolate and solaced the bruised heart's dumb agony; and – some mock.

> Loud mockers in the roaring street
> Say Christ is crucified again:
> Twice pierced His gospel-bearing feet,
> Twice broken His great heart in vain.
> I hear, and to myself I smile,
> For Christ talks with me all the while.[14]

In the city of Smyrna, about the year 160, while Statius Quadratus was Roman proconsul, there occurred a frightful martyrdom. The aged Polycarp, bishop and saint, was brought to his trial. His judge stood before him and cried: 'You are to renounce the faith! You are to curse the name of Christ!'

But Polycarp gave answer: 'Fourscore and six years have I served him, and he never did me wrong; how then can I revile my King, my Saviour?'

So they took him and burned him to death in the amphitheatre.

But the young church in Smyrna hurled its defiance in the face of his murderers; for when they came to write down in the annals of the church what had happened, they were very careful to put in the precise date, and then they gave it thus: 'Polycarp was martyred, Statius Quadratus being proconsul of Asia, and *Jesus Christ being King for ever.*'

These defiant words can be echoed today from every corner of the globe, for the heel of the persecutor still rests upon the throat of the church. To cite but one example, Wang Mingdao, a leader of the underground church in China, and referred to as the Nelson Mandela of Chinese Christianity, was imprisoned for nearly twenty-four years during the period of Maoist domination. During all this time he resisted the insidious and repeated attempts to force him to renounce his faith. Asked in interview what had been most important to him in his time in prison, he replied, 'The Word, the Word!', and then broke into the words of 'Onward! Christian Soldiers':[15]

> Crowns and thrones may perish,
> Kingdoms rise and wane,
> But the church of Jesus
> Constant will remain . . .

> 'Glory, laud and honour
> Unto *Christ the King!*'
> This through countless ages
> Men and angels sing.

'Jesus is Lord.' That is the faith!

These three features of contemporary life which we have identified – diversity, unity, and the Lordship of Christ – are of course, additionally, the three factors that combine in the Ephesians 1:10 revelation of God's purpose: all things together under Christ.

But this polarized, diversity-in-unity world under the reign of Christ which we are presently inhabiting is actually not a 'first'. In fact, *at least once before in history, that very pattern expressed itself – the world into which the gospel came in the beginning.* So we now reconsider the world into which the Christian church was born.

In so doing the thread of our argument is not lost, but actually is significantly reinforced. Why? Because, assuming we can credibly establish a meaningful parallel between the first- and twenty-first-century worlds, the remarkable fruitfulness of the good news of Jesus Christ in the first century will imply exciting possibilities of a similar effectiveness in our own time, for a church that is prepared to become the modern equivalent of the instrument God used so effectively in the first century – a diversity-in-unity, 'together under Christ' community.

# 5 It's happened before

*The first-century world*

## The Greco-Roman Empire

The Greco-Roman world of the first century may not unfairly be described as 'skin over cracks'. The 'skin' was the Empire. Roman empire-building assumed a quite specific form, one which actually distinguished it from all the great world empires that had successively dominated the Mediterranean and ancient Near Eastern worlds over the centuries of civilization.

As its legions pushed outwards in all directions, Rome expanded its rule, and new territories with their native populations were constantly added to its dominion. However, as scholars have noted, there was little attempt in most cases to absorb these tribal peoples into a full Roman identity. 'The solidarity of the Empire was a product of the sheer preponderance of Roman might rather than of direct centralized administration.'[1]

Not that Rome was less than utterly ruthless in imposing her will if called upon. But she learned how to blend the sheer 'will to power' with a certain sensitivity to local aspirations. 'The secret of Rome's success where others had failed lay in her wise provision for differing kinds of local supervision and control.'[2]

## Skin over cracks

Patently, there were the overarching features, the 'skin', to use the earlier image, represented by military dominance, law and (some) institutions, a formal language (Latin), a common language (koine Greek), a network of roads, and a religious veneer over an almost endless pluralism (the emperor cult). But the Empire in general consisted in a mosaic rather than a melting-pot; under this 'skin' lay a massive diversity of ethnicity, language, race and culture. The 'skin' was critical, however, for the effective spread of the Christian faith, as it provided the highways of communication by which the gospel could rapidly spread as well as the means for travel and interpersonal contacts.

But the 'skin' did something else. It created a mindset, it stirred a longing, it awakened a dream at the horizons of imagination, which projected the individual beyond purely personal and tribal boundaries. It vivified a longing deeply set in every human heart for a larger world of harmony and peace, where ancient hatreds and rivalries would be buried for ever, and swords would become ploughshares, and spears pruning-hooks, and wars would be no more, and neighbour-love would extend across human borders and reach as far and wide as the human family.

Thus a certain general parallel can be drawn between the present world of the early third millennium and the world into which the gospel first came. The third feature we noted earlier with respect to today's world was also a feature then – the lordship of Jesus Christ. To cite one representative example from the New Testament: as Stephen was dying under the hail of rocks outside Jerusalem, he was heard to cry out, 'I see heaven open and the Son of Man standing at the right hand of God' (Acts 7:56). It was precisely that vision, and the theological conviction that lay at the heart of it concerning the resurrection and enthronement of Jesus, which inspired the apostles in their tireless witness and enabled them to prevail against the most incredible odds which were ranged against them.

For these disciples of Jesus in the first century, as for the disciples of Jesus all over the world in the twenty-first century, Jesus reigns.

To return to the first-century world, it is surely not surprising that in that environment of intense diversity, often marked by conflict – yet alongside the trappings of wider horizons – one of the major attractions of Christianity, as writers universally conclude, was its offer of community. 'Perhaps this was the way in which the gospel made its deepest impression on the pagan world.'[3]

Kenneth Scott Latourette, in his monumental history of the church, notes the way the great apologists for the faith were able to appeal to the Christians' lifestyles in vindication of their claims for Christ:

> They placed great weight on the moral transformation wrought by the Gospel, and contrasted with the pagan society about them the high character of the Christian community, the fashion in which Christians helped one another, and the bringing together in one peaceable fellowship of those different tribes and customs who had formerly hated one another.[4]

### An embodied question mark

In John Poulton's memorable words, referring to the specific case of the slave–master relationship but aptly conveying the universal significance of early Christian, new-humanity community:

> When masters could call slaves brothers, and when the enormities of depersonalizing them became conscious in enough people's minds, something had to go. It took time, but slavery went. And in the interim, the people of God were an embodied question mark, because here were some people who could live *another set of relationships within the given social system.*[5]

An 'embodied question mark', living 'another set of relationships within the given social system' – in which the different other was embraced instead of rejected, loved instead of hated, regarded as a brother or sister instead of an enemy, within a new kind of human existence which was destined to inherit the world – such was the heartbeat of the first-century church.

After the breakdown of the Empire (from the fifth to the ninth centuries), first in the West and then the East, the imperial 'skin' was shredded, and peoples retreated behind the walls of nation states, where they remained until the modern period. Accordingly, it is arguable that in some important senses it is not until the twenty-first century, not until the arrival of the world that surrounds us today, that the 'skin' has regrown in terms of present-day globalization. Thus, for the first time since the first century, we have a recovery of certain primary contextual features of the environment in which Christianity made such impressive headway in the beginning.

## A striking parallel

The point I am making here is that there is a striking parallel between the world of the first century, with its massive local diversities and its imperial 'global' skin, and the twenty-first-century, third-millennium world in which we live today, with its unprecedented 'in your face' diversities and its globalization skin.

Now, admittedly, the brush strokes here are very broad indeed, and, unless my initial biblical section was invalid, the case for the new-humanity congregation most certainly does not hang on the validity of the parallel. However, the parallels noted in the last two paragraphs are interesting, to say the least, and surely merit thoughtful pondering.

Here again is huge social diversity with a unifying 'skin' which forces people to come to terms, whether they want to or not, with the 'different' human neighbours all around them. But the 'skin' can once again provide a facility for communication across the various gulfs and contradictions, and, critically, it establishes a human context that affords a massive opportunity, as it did in the first century, for a message that can offer authentic human community in the midst of it all.

## The community crisis

The urgent significance of this parallel is today being underlined, for, under the 'skin', the expanding diversity is spawning serious outbreaks of communal antagonism and ethnic conflict right across the world, not least in the old Western 'homelands'.

Alvin Toffler warns:

> The sudden shift of social ground-rules today, the smudging of roles, status distinctions, and lines of authority, the immersion in blip culture, and above all the break-up of the great thought system, indust-reality, have shattered the world-image most of us carry around in our skulls.

In consequence, most people surveying the world around them today see only chaos. They suffer a sense of personal powerlessness and pointlessness.[6]

Further:

A society fast fragmenting at the level of values and lifestyles challenges all the old integrative mechanisms and cries out for a totally new basis for reconstitution. We have by no means yet found this basis. Yet if we shall face disturbing, agonizing problems of social integration, we shall confront even more agonizing problems of individual integration. For the multiplication of lifestyles challenges our ability to hold the very self together.[7]

'We have by no means yet found this totally new basis for reconstruction': this is the view of Toffler, the secular prophet, but it surely resonates with every Christian with a missionary heart.

### Required: a new kind of human

Interestingly, but hardly surprisingly, precisely this dilemma was faced by early Marxist thought. Responding to Feuerbach's claim, 'We need new men!', Marx wrote, 'Only when the real, individual man ... as an individual human being has become a *species-being* [i.e. a social being] in his everyday life, in his particular work, in his particular situation ... only then will human emancipation have been accomplished.'[8] But when the Marxist revolution of 1917 failed to deliver this new breed of humans, this 'social' man, Lenin was faced with exactly this dilemma. The Achilles' heel of Marxism is exposed at precisely this point. 'The weakness of the Marxists seems to be that they have overlooked the fact that the changing of [social] conditions is a necessary, but not a sufficient condition for producing the new humanity.'[9]

I recall a business friend during the Communist period in Russia recounting how, in the course of a working visit to Moscow, he and his colleagues had been taken from their hotel to a lecture on the superior virtues of Marxism – only to discover on returning to their rooms that their shirts had been stolen during their absence. Not that similar thefts do not regularly occur under capitalism. But it neatly illustrates the point being made here, that the real need, whatever the social conditions, is for a power to overcome the cupidity of the human heart.

Humanist Walter Lippmann uttered identical sentiments in the aftermath of the Second World War: 'We ourselves were so sure that at long last the generation had arisen, keen and eager, to put this disorderly earth to right, and fit to do it. We meant so well, we tried so hard, and look what we have made of it. We can only muddle into muddle. *What is required is a new kind of man.*'[10]

The crisis of the third millennium is a crisis of community, the need for a new kind of persons united in a new kind of society. The great towering issue before us today, the issue that transcends all others and thrusts itself more and more to the head of every agenda for humanity's future survival and progress, is this: how are we to live in peace, tolerance and harmony with our 'different' neighbours? The dreams of the ages for a better world come down to this – no, more than that, the very hope for human survival on planet Earth comes down to this: where can I find a loving neighbour? And how can I myself be a loving neighbour to others? The answers from the seers quoted above are uniform in their pessimism. And is there any truly convincing evidence to be found anywhere, in a single daily newspaper, or a single television newscast, that they are not entirely justified in their hopelessness? On the assumption that we have to construct our solution, our ideal person, our new humanity, out of the raw material of fallen human nature, the quest is doomed.

The world, in other words, has no answer to the deepening social crisis of our time, no means of holding together in living community the diversities of our burgeoning, multi-faceted cultures. And yet find such a means it must, for the global forces driving these diversities into ever-closer confrontation are irreversible.

## There is an answer

'We have by no means yet found this totally new basis for reconstruction.' But the witness of history, as reflected in Christianity's foundational documents, is that in the parallel world of the first century there emerged groups of people, scattered throughout the Empire, who *had* discovered a totally new basis for social reconstruction, and lived it out, as an 'embodied question mark', before the watching world in their local Christian congregations.

Moreover, despite the limitations to which they constantly drew attention, they did it to such effect that multitudes were drawn as by a magnet to share in their discovery. But we have that answer still available to us today, lying on the surface of the New Testament – the gospel, the great good news of Jesus Christ.

What a moment of opportunity this represents for the Christian message! What a profoundly relevant vision this generates for our local churches, all across the globe, to become, through the grace and power of God, places of community; bridging points amid all the diversities and polarizations of human cultures; centres of reconciliation with God and our neighbours; families of love. If we do so, I dare to believe that the world will once again come running to share in the blessings.

# 6  Widening the view

*Other dimensions of community*

Up to this point we have confined our application of the Bible's concern for community to the local Christian congregation. That is entirely defensible in terms of the concentration of the New Testament. The local church will accordingly remain our primary focus. However, there are other kinds of community which are also important when considering the ministry of the local congregation. We pause in this chapter to give attention to them.

## The inner community

In his stimulating exploration of higher education today, Parker J. Palmer notes the indissoluble connection between the 'external community' of a classroom and the 'internal community' that the individual student, or the individual teacher, has within himself or herself. 'Community cannot take root in a divided life. Long before community assumes external shape and form it must be present as seed in the undivided self; only as we are in communion can we find community with others.'[1]

This important insight has clear biblical support. The Genesis picture of humanity before the fall has clear indications of an individual wholeness and integration. The statement that 'God created human beings in his own image' (Gen. 1:27) necessarily implies, among many things, God's mirroring in his creature his own essential unity of being and identity, caught in the words of the Hebrew *Shema*: 'Hear, O Israel: the LORD our God, the LORD is one' (Deut. 6:4; cf. Mark 12:29).

The further affirmation that 'God blessed them' (Gen. 1:28) surely implies in Adam and Eve an integrated sense of themselves, expressed in their free and uninhibited communion with God (2:15–25), a communion undisturbed by the fact of human moral responsibility (2:16–17), and marked additionally in the observation that 'the man and his wife . . . felt no shame' (2:25).

The presentation of the fall that follows centres on the serpent's allurement, and specifically on his promise, 'You will be like God, knowing good and evil' (3:5). The immediate effect of Adam and Eve's primal rebellion against God's good and loving will is a disturbing self-awareness of their physical nakedness, an inner shame, and a dread of God: 'The man and his wife . . . hid from the LORD God among the trees of the garden' (3:8).

### War within

Thus sin brought internal disruption and conflict. The former internal harmony, the fruit of a God-centred consciousness, is replaced by a self-centred, internal dis-ease. Paul depicts this in graphic terms in Romans: 'When I want to do good sin is right there with me. For in my inner being I delight in God's law; but I see another law at work in the members of my body, waging war against the law of my mind and making me a prisoner . . . For what I want to do I do not do, but what I hate I do . . . What a wretched man I am!' (7:21–23, 15, 24).

Robert Louis Stephenson caught this experience of internal conflict in his classic tale *Dr Jekyll and Mr Hyde*. The kind, respectable medical practitioner, Dr Jekyll, falls under the spell of a drug that transforms him into the vicious, depraved and deformed Mr Hyde. As his life spirals towards final destruction, Dr Jekyll explains that he has learned that man is not truly one, but two; 'that in the agonized womb of consciousness these polar twins should be continuously struggling'. Stephenson later wrote to a friend: 'Jekyll is a dreadful thing I own.' Its subject matter, he confided, was really 'that old business of the war in the members'.[2] For Pascal, similarly, man is 'an embodied paradox, a bundle of contradictions'.[3]

Because of the incursion of sin, human nature is internally at war, pulled in different directions; a place of incurable restlessness. 'The wicked are like the tossing sea, which cannot rest ... "There is no peace," says my God, "for the wicked"' (Isa. 57:20–21).

Granted this universal reality of the divided self, it is no surprise that true community has proved such a frail bloom in the garden of human history.

### A new centre

Across the centuries, Christian community has seemed at times comparably elusive, but happily it also has its story of achievement. Begun in the wonder of the Pentecost experience, where 'they were all together' and 'devoted themselves ... to the fellowship'; when 'all the believers were one in heart and mind', and 'shared everything they had' (Acts 2:1, 42; 4:32), it continued, during the early Christian centuries, in the quality of mutual commitment which has been documented in the previous chapter. It is to be experienced still in a multitude of churches in every corner of the earth.

The basis for this experience of authentic interpersonal communion lies in the inner unification that is instigated in the human heart by its rebirth through the Holy Spirit. God comes again to the centre of a human life and reclaims his throne in the self. We become people 'in Christ' whose identity is affected by our union of life with the exalted Jesus: 'I have been crucified with Christ and I no longer live, but Christ lives in me. The life I live in the body, I live by faith in the Son of God' (Gal. 2:20).

The finality of this new standing in union with Christ is to be affirmed here and now for all who believe in him as Lord and Saviour (Gal. 2:20; Rom. 6:1–11; 7:1–6; 8:1–30; etc.). However, the re-formation of the individual around its new centre in Christ is a progressive thing (Rom. 6:19; 1 Cor. 15:31; 2 Cor. 3:18; 4:10; Eph. 4:15; Phil. 3:10–14; Col. 3:10), promoted not least, according to Jesus, by the impact of God's Word (John 17:17; cf. 2 Tim. 3:16; Rom. 6:4–11), the supreme instrument of God's Spirit in his work of renewing God's people, and restoring to them a unified self-awareness centred on God himself.

Here, Palmer's insight that only as we are in communion within ourselves can we be in communion with others affects our new-humanity vision. Local churches that hope to experience the new humanity in Christ need to give a central place in their life, worship and ministries to the exposition and application of Scripture. But as this happens they will begin to experience that renewal of the inner person that makes them the raw material of tangible, loving community which, in measure, mirrors the unity of the Father and the Son (John 17:21–23), and which will 'let the world know that you sent me' (verse 23).

### A family of hope

However, the relationship between the two kinds of community is more complex than a simple matter of cause (the achievement of internal communion) producing the effect (the achievement of external communion). The movement is also, to an extent, in the other direction.

Joan's story illustrates this very well.

My growing years were within a very dysfunctional family. My only memories were of verbal, physical, emotional and sexual abuse, in a family heavily involved in the occult. Sadly, I knew nothing of the love of God and was unaware that he was with me during these lost years … In 1972, after my first suicide attempt, I started questioning my life … Then on a significant day in 1984, feeling that my whole life was coming apart, I pleaded to this God to give me a proof of his existence.

What an experience! He immediately removed all fear of claustrophobia that I had suffered with since traumatic episodes in childhood. Then, like Thomas, I could say, 'My Lord and my God.' That same year with the help of loving Christians I experienced my first holy communion and knew its true meaning. I was ready to receive baptism that April. The Lord helped me to continue growing and to become fully aware that he was always with me.

The full journey back started on a day when I was 'screaming' for help, and the Lord led me to the Vancouver Christian Counselling Centre. Through gentle, prayerful counselling I was slowly able to expose my true self to another person … and the healing began. In August 1990, I crept into the back pew of First Baptist [Church] and I knew I had come into my safe harbour. It was as if I were the only person there, and the words given by God through the preacher that morning were spoken directly to me. The love and caring of the church family has given me back my life. I know that I am his beloved child and that through the prayer of my Christian family the bondage of Satan is broken. Like the butterfly emerging from the cocoon, I am truly free.

Joan's experience highlights the important qualifier we noted a moment ago: the achieving of a truly integrated personhood in Jesus Christ, and the experience of Christian community, are commonly not two successive steps so much as two ongoing processes which mutually interact. Joan experienced the blessing of a healing community, and was able eventually to contribute to it, out of her new 'centred' life in Christ. It is in fact partly through our brokenness and sense of need that we are able to enter into community in the first place. When we discover, as Joan did, the wonder of the grace of a God who accepts us as we are, from that root grows the ability to face ourselves in our brokenness and to trust ourselves to others. People who have no sense of their inner need are typically unable to relate at depth to others. It is in our experience of common vulnerability and failure that we find a place of meeting, a place of fellowship and community.

Henri Nouwen confirms this insight: 'Every time I am willing to break out of my false needs for self-sufficiency, and dare to ask for help, a new community emerges – a fellowship of the weak – strong in the trust that together we can be a people of hope in a broken world.'[4]

A congregation that has learned the meaning of grace, and begun to live by it, will be a congregation where the 'communion of the Holy Spirit' will be an inevitable and authentic experience.

## The outer community

Community in the local church is affected not only internally by the harmony (or lack of it) within the self, but also externally by the congregation's relationships with other church communities. Congregations do not exist in isolation. Rather, they are tiny parts of a vastly greater whole – the sum total of all the people of God, spread all around the world (our part in the 'worship wave') – and also spread through all the ages, one day to be gathered 'as a radiant church, without stain or wrinkle or any other blemish, but holy and blameless' (Eph. 5:27), in the presence of the Lord Jesus Christ at his glorious appearing.

### These pesky Baptists . . . or Anglicans . . . or Pentecostals . . .
The fact of our communion with the church of all the ages will be addressed in the discussion of worship in the next chapter. Our relationship with the global church, and in particular with other Christians and other churches that meet for worship in our neighbourhood, or to whom we may have historic, present denominational ties, needs consideration at this point. In its widest terms it is our relationship with our fellow participants in the weekly 'worship wave' we celebrated in the Introduction. It is one thing to join, delightfully, every Sunday with the one to two billion other worshippers of the triune God as the song of praise goes round the earth; but it is another thing to ask the potentially awkward question of how we relate to other groups of Christians when they assume the form of the congregation on the neighbouring corner or at the end of our road.

That such relationships are not a concern of him who is Head and Lord of all Christian people is surely unthinkable. Jesus' prayer for the unity of his people removes any lingering question (John 17:20–23). Patently, it was, and is, and will be, his personal concern. Accordingly, it ought also to be ours. The fact that there are by general computation some 22,000 Christian denominations or their equivalent worldwide is a matter of grave scandal when we consider the prayer of Jesus or the unity of the Godhead.[5]

Today there is general recognition that the New Testament's focus on the specific, local congregation has great merit in promoting the cause of Christ, the spread of the gospel and the up-building both of individual Christian lives and of authentic Christian community. New-humanity congregations are expressions of that frame of reference.

Extra-congregational ties and connections should not, however, be ignored – witness the prayer of Jesus. Denominations are commonly seen today as having only a limited shelf life; however, at very least, they provide a sense of identity and belonging, a family of kindred congregations who meet every church's need for accountability, the needed supports for leadership ministry, and channels for global mission and humanitarian action.

In the New Testament, unity is never exalted to the point that all other considerations are eliminated. Jesus shared a whole theological tradition with the Pharisees and teachers of the law in his native Palestine. Yet that did not inhibit him from demonstrating with great candour the shortcomings of these groups (cf. Matt. 12:1–14; 15:1–14; 21:23–46; 23:1–39; Mark 11:12–18; Luke 11:14–54; 18:9–14; John 8:12–59; 10:22–23). Paul, similarly, was in no mood to extend overtures of unity towards his judaizing opponents. The fact that they also claimed to be Christians, and to have authentic credentials, did nothing to exculpate them (Gal. 1:8–9 and *passim*; 2 Cor. 11:1–15). John is identically inflexible in his dismissal of the proto-gnostic teachers in his day, who denied the true incarnation of God in Jesus (1 John 2:18–19; 4:1–3), despite the fact, as we know from recently discovered Nag Hammadi writings, that many of them claimed to have a personal relationship with Christ.

Thus there is no obligation laid upon us to develop close ties with those who either deny the fundamentals of the faith or promote lifestyles that Scripture asserts to be dishonouring to God and opposed to his good will for his creatures.

## Together under Christ

Happily, in many communities around the world there are opportunities for genuine sharing with fellow Christians where neither heterodox beliefs nor unscriptural lifestyle practices raise problems. In such circumstances Scripture would encourage us to reach out to one another without fear.

J. I. Packer and Thomas C. Oden have demonstrated the fact of 'an evangelical consensus', a common matrix of beliefs on major biblical and theological themes, such as the supreme authority of Holy Scripture, belief in the one triune God, the creation and the fall, the divine–human person and the saving work of Jesus Christ, justification by grace through faith, the sending of the Holy Spirit, the church as the sent-forth people of God, and the second coming of Christ.[6] Where such truths are joyfully affirmed, we should be in the vanguard of promoting expressions and opportunities for fellowship and other forms of shared testimony.[7]

*What have you that you did not receive?*
One other way to promote inter-congregational fellowship, particularly on the local level, is to admit to, and deal with before God, our feeling of threat from other church groups and ministry leaders. Ordained clergy and pastors are particularly prone to this unhelpful attitude. We are often much too possessive of our congregations, fearful that contact with others might lead to their being 'stolen' from our flock, secretly ashamed of the moderate 'success' of our work, and inappropriately jealous of the gifts and status of our brothers and sisters in ministry. We too readily forget that every servant of God is tried and struggling much of the time, and that all gifts of ministry are in fact 'gifts' that belong to all God's people (not merely to the one graced with them), and which are finally for the honour of the Lord.

Where such barriers can be overcome, new-humanity congregations ought to be in the vanguard of this wider fellowship and open to the enrichment it can bring to their own lives and communities.

## The linguistic community: the challenge of language

In the first century, the comprehensiveness of the congregations in the Greco-Roman world was greatly aided by the fact of a virtually universal language of communication, koine Greek. To that fact we owe the speedy dissemination of the gospel and the creation of the New Testament.

Today such uniformity eludes us. The curse of the tower of Babel (Gen. 11:1–9) still hangs over the globe. Pentecost was a salutary foretaste of God's future gift of universal language communication when those of every language under heaven are depicted as united in a common song of praise (Rev. 7:9–10). The Holy Spirit's gift of tongues is a further pointer forward to that dreamed-of linguistic paradise. For the present, and until Christ returns, diversity of language is the reality. Since the ability to articulate meaningfully and communicate linguistically is basic to human relationships, difference of language means that not all Christians will find a place in the same congregation. To that extent the vision of the new-humanity church needs to be modified. However, several comments are in order.

### Broader than ethnicity

Firstly, the whole thrust of this book is that new-humanity communities are not concerned merely with issues of racial or ethnic integration. The New Testament evidence is clear that *all* human diversities are to be addressed and overcome in authentic new-humanity congregations. Thus a congregation that organizes itself in separation because of language still faces major challenges at other points of human divisiveness, such as gender, generation, socio-economic levels, physical and mental health, family units and personality type. Hence new-humanity principles continue to be highly relevant to its relational life.

Secondly, the new-humanity principles which we have spelled out from Scripture are relevant to the vast majority of church contexts globally. A common local language prevails and allows for the formation of biblically mandated, inclusive congregations across racial and ethnic lines.

Thirdly, in many other cases the arrival of new generations in a new country creates the option of embracing the language of the country of adoption. Thus many immigrant denominations in various parts of the world have, with time, simply merged with parent denominations in the welcoming nation. The period of overlap is not easy, but if the goal is clear, and Christian love prevails, appropriate accommodations can be made while the congregation is in linguistic transition.

### A gift from God

Fourthly, biblically understood, no language is eternally sacrosanct; it is a gift from our Creator, and much that gives us identity gathers around it and flows from it. In an initial period of adjustment to a new country, with its attendant insecurities, our language of origin provides a welcome and necessary place of familiarity and security. But, for all of us, our language is not of ultimate value; it too may need to be offered to God in the 'living sacrifice' which his cross requires of us all (Rom. 12:1–2; 2 Cor. 5:15). Thus, at a certain stage, the challenge of adopting the language of a country of adoption may need to be courageously faced.

### As a living sacrifice

The sacrifice at this point can be very real, especially if our coming to Christ has been in our own language. Adapting our personal faith and its deeper emotions to new words in a different tongue may feel like losing something very precious. However, for the sake of the kingdom and the glory of God through his church, the attempt may need to be made, and its long-term fruit in freeing the next generation to find authentic language in which to encounter Christ, and thereafter to serve him, will bring its own reward.

Fifthly, when ethnic congregations, typically of newer immigrants, are gathered around a particular language other than the language of the host culture, it is not uncommon for them to use another church's building. In such cases the biblical norm of multi-ethnic, multi-racial unity can be given expression through regular activities that unite the two (or more) congregations, and even make possible periodic united worship services. Church membership in such cases can be of a single 'congregation' until such time as the whole community has sufficient linguistic commonality to become one church. Translation facilities, in these days of advanced communication technologies, can also help to bridge the gap period and allow the multi-ethnic witness of the church to be increasingly expressed.

### Mono-ethnic congregations

Finally, a particular language-related issue is that of congregations that are consciously created as mono-ethnic, and accordingly operate entirely in their first, 'native' language, irrespective of the language spoken in the surrounding host culture.

In many parts of the world where the gospel is penetrating new cultures and language groups not previously reached with the Christian faith, a concentration upon their first language is the obvious initial stage in mission. It will be many years in many such cases before any wider inclusiveness can be contemplated.

But the mono-ethnic congregation is also a worldwide phenomenon in settings that have a long history of Christian faith and witness. Particularly impressive examples are Chinese and Korean congregations, which continue to spring up all around the globe, ministering to Chinese and Korean communities. These congregations often show a dynamism and growth rate significantly beyond those in the surrounding parent cultures. How does the new-humanity model relate in these cases?

There is often a 'generation gap' issue in these churches. While the older generation are happy to remain in a Chinese, Korean or other 'native' language form, the younger second generation in many cases prefer to adopt, and express their faith and their lives in, the language and cultural milieu of their country of adoption.

The resolving of potential conflict by developing separate generational congregations within the one church may provide some degree of short-term resolution, but it suffers from the major liability that both groups lack the vital input of the other. The long-term result is also highly regrettable, as the 'senior congregation' experiences, with time, a diminishing vitality as well as diminishing size, and finds itself increasingly isolated from the surrounding culture.

While combining the two generations in one congregation is fraught with many challenges, it would appear to be a better solution in the long term, and certainly a model patently better able to express the values of unity in diversity which we have identified and celebrated throughout this book.

### To all nations

Moreover, while the embrace of a single cultural inheritance, including a single native language, no doubt has many attractions and promotes the vitality of these congregations in the short term, there needs to be an openness also to listen to the summons of Scripture to a trans-ethnic inclusivism.

A leader of an English-teaching operation in China remarked recently on the need he was sensing to urge his Chinese Christian friends to move beyond a vision confined to the native Chinese population and face the challenge of reaching the vast numbers of tribal peoples within the Chinese provinces, who speak their own languages of origin, and who in many cases have as yet no Christian believers among them.

Every Christian congregation, without exception, needs to embrace the Great Commission of Jesus, which lays responsibility from the Head and Lord of every church to 'make disciples of all nations'. Accordingly, mono-cultural congregations, while clearly blessed by God in many places, would be wise to recognize that, from the perspective of the global witness of the church, they are a temporary rather then a permanent form of congregational life, and to anticipate a time when, as God opens their hearts and eyes to the needy multitudes around their churches from *all* nations, and as God uses them to lead such folk to Christ, their churches will find themselves widening their mission and ministry to become multi-ethnic, multi-racial and multi-cultural, as were the congregations of the New Testament.

But the good news is that such a development is an advance, not a retreat, and holds in promise all kinds of new Holy Spirit blessings. Such inclusiveness will, of course, also prepare the congregation for the coming community of glory, when all will be one in the presence of him who comes as Head of the church and Lord of all.

# 7 Down to earth

*Worship and leadership in the new-humanity church*

To this point the case has been rooted in Scripture, buttressed in the last few chapters by an appeal to history. Even if the theory is correct, and hence new-humanity, diversity-in-unity, together-under-Christ congregations are truly the way to go, there emerges a host of practical considerations. How does this model work out in the trenches of day-to-day congregational life? We shall address five primary areas in turn. Later in the chapter we shall consider leadership, and subsequent chapters will look at discipleship, fellowship and mission, all in a new-humanity context. We begin, however, with worship, the very heart of any Christian community.

## WORSHIP

However persuasive the case for an inclusive congregational model may be at the biblical, theological and historical levels, the practical difficulties faced in keeping all the diversities together are likely to be a turn-off for many people. Nowhere is this more so than in the area of worship. The challenge, at the racial level, is caught by Nancy, a white Presbyterian woman. 'Because of our cultural backgrounds, [blacks and whites] might not enjoy the same kinds of worship. The way we express our worship to God is different. And so if I choose to worship in the way I enjoy worshipping, and my black brothers and sisters want to worship in another fashion, that should be okay.' Today's emergence of generational churches is largely driven by the same attitude. 'Our tastes in music are so different, it's just "worship wars" if we try to worship together.'[1]

What gives distinctive shape to worship in a new-humanity church?

## All members of the congregation worship together

Paul's letter to the Romans is, among other things, a sustained appeal for the unity of the Jewish and Gentile factions in the church in Rome. He establishes the theological basis of this unity in the early chapters, arguing that all alike, Jew and Gentile, are 'under sin' (1:18 – 3:20), and that all alike, Jew and Gentile, are saved from sin's consequences only by the grace of God expressed in the atoning sacrifice of Jesus Christ (3:21 – 6:23).

### One heart and one voice

In the important 'So what?' section in Romans 15:1–13, he expounds the implications of these shared realities: in general 'a spirit of unity among yourselves as you follow Christ' (verse 5), and in particular a shared experience of worship: 'Therefore I [as a Jew] will praise you among the Gentiles; I will sing hymns to your name'; 'Praise the Lord, all you Gentiles, and sing praises to him, all you peoples' (i.e. Jews and Gentiles together); and, most explicit of all, '. . . that with one heart and mouth you may glorify the God and Father of our Lord Jesus Christ' (Rom. 15:9, quoting 2 Sam. 22:50 and Ps. 18:49; Rom. 15:11, quoting Ps. 117:1; Rom. 15:6).

The worship of the one people of God is to be expressed as the 'one people' who meet in one place and one time. Without intending to be inappropriately judgmental, it is frankly difficult to see how this biblical principle is upheld in congregations that divide into generational or other sub-sections for their corporate worship. An authentic church in New Testament terms is a group of Christians who regularly and consciously worship as a total community.

## No-one is disenfranchised in worship

This second principle is essentially a teasing-out of the first one. New-humanity churches are based on the biblical estimate of human dignity. If, as Genesis 1:27 states, all humans are made 'in the image of God', and if as, 1 John 2:2 states, Jesus Christ has made 'the atoning sacrifice for . . . the sins of the whole world', then patently every single person in God's world is a being of infinite worth. Whenever they live, wherever they live, and in whatever circumstances, they are authentic members of that race of creatures who were made as the Creator's image-bearers, and are the personal objects of divine love as demonstrated in the self-sacrifice of the Son of God upon the cross. All are of inestimable value.

### Worship for all

Accordingly, there are no sub-classes of people, no sub-classes of Christians, and, emphatically, no sub-classes of Christian worshippers. Every worshipper is of equal worth, called to present a worship offering in the sight of God that is of equal value to that of all other worshippers. Hence each worshipper has an equal claim to a worship experience with which they will be able to meaningfully identify, and which will be an authentic vehicle of their worship.

This principle is obviously violated in services where the needs of a particular generation are permitted a dominant role. But no-one can be disenfranchised in worship without there being a dishonouring of the God who made and redeemed them. Worship therefore needs to be consciously shaped so that *all* members of the congregation can experience it as a generally meaningful vehicle for their response to God.

In practice, with the use of a little imagination, places can be found for supplementary worship experiences where sub-sets of the congregation can meet and express worship in a manner that is entirely of one style. During our ministry in Vancouver, opportunities for peer worship occurred in the weekly youth meeting and as an elective during evening-service options, and the seniors could enjoy a 'hymn sing' as part of their regular get-togethers. Among our small groups was one where 'charismatic gifts' were expressed, without that overriding the more ordered worship style preferred by the rest of the church, and an annual 'old-fashioned singalong' service gave the entire congregation, if they wished it, access to a solid diet of older songs. In other words, a generally integrated form for the whole congregation together need not exclude more focused forms around its periphery.

## Worship must 'please our neighbour' as well as ourselves

> We who are strong ought to bear with the failings of the weak and not to please ourselves. We should all please our neighbours for their good, to build them up. For even Christ did not please himself (Rom. 15:1–2).

Putting this another way, in worship none of us can get *all* that they want. During my pastorate in Vancouver I learned the wisdom of clarifying this biblical principle. It involved saying to every aspiring church member, 'If you are looking for a church that will give you everything you want, then don't become a member here at First Baptist. But if you are looking for a church that will give you *most* of what you want, but also a chance to grow with others who are different from yourself, then this is the church for you. And, incidentally, you will be in great shape for heaven!'

### Good for everybody

Over many years, and meeting hundreds of aspiring members, I never had a single refusal. However, this critically important principle of all church membership was established at the outset: church is not primarily about what *I* want, and what suits me and my family, but about what is good for *everybody*. The church should actually be the one group in every community where that principle is lived out in its fullest terms.

This principle of 'dying' to what pleases me is of course enshrined for ever in the biblical rite of entry to the church – Christian baptism, which Paul expounded earlier in Romans (cf. 6:1–23). Irrespective of whether the rite is administered in promissory terms in early infancy, or in experiential terms to those who are professing personal faith in Christ in later years, the meaning is the same. We 'die with Christ' and are 'raised with him' to a radically new kind of living characterized by the ending of self-centredness and the beginning of a new love of our neighbour (cf. Rom. 6:1–23; Gal. 2:20; 3:26–29, leading to 5:22–26 and 6:10; Col. 2:11–12, leading to 3:9–14).

Accordingly, worship occasions in a new-humanity church will be consciously structured in a way that facilitates the worship of *all sections* of the congregation who gather. It will also allow the members to learn, through the diversity of the forms and styles encompassed, to accept and honour their Christian sisters and brothers, and hence grow further in the path of likeness to him who 'did not please himself'. Christ-like worship, while fully realizable only in the life to come, surely remains the universal goal of all our worship here; and that means worship that includes rather than excludes, which reaches out, after the model of Jesus, to embrace all, rather than to cater to a sub-section of a congregation.

### Knowing the flock

It is an obvious practical corollary of this third principle that those who are responsible for shaping the worship experience week by week are in vital contact with the *whole* congregation, and aware of their needs and concerns. The practice of delegating this responsibility solely to musicians, however well trained and gifted, appears to misunderstand the communal basis of worship. Obviously a musical awareness and expertise is a most valuable contribution to the process, but it can never be the only criterion. Every act of Christian worship should arise out of the life of the believing congregation, and hence be shaped by those who are in ongoing contact with the people of God who gather for the worship service.

The frequently experienced sense of disenfranchisement of either the younger or the older members of a congregation is not truly or healthily addressed by dividing the congregation along generational lines. That route appears replete with unbiblical instincts. Worship that 'suits me' or 'enables my generation to worship', at the expense of the unity of the body, and in violation of the ministry of God the Holy Spirit, who has actually made us all one in Jesus Christ, can hardly claim biblical support. Furthermore, such generational worship eliminates the true mutuality and richness of a congregational experience where, in the terms of Paul's analogy of the body in 1 Corinthians 12, the older part of a congregation cannot say to the younger, 'I don't need you', and vice versa. 'On the contrary, those parts of the body that seem to be weaker are indispensable' (1 Cor. 12:21–22).[2]

The new-humanity way accepts, and celebrates with delight, the diversity that God gives us in calling those from all generations, all races, all ethnicities and all social spheres, to be part of the unique, supernatural community of the body of Christ.

### God is really among you!

The reference to the 'supernatural' here is critical. Christian worship must not be shaped by the findings of sociology as to what people 'prefer' or 'need', but rather by God the Holy Spirit. Christian worship needs to be sociologically *inexplicable*, not sociologically conformist. It should reflect the new order of the kingdom of God, where relationships become possible that surrounding society can never achieve. It should and can become a community where we learn to love one another in our diversity, and to discover, through the struggles and the maturing of these relationships, a new form of life together that is wonderfully satisfying, truly honouring to the Lord, and, moreover, as we shall note in a later chapter, highly potent evangelistically.

Perhaps only then shall we see the regular replication of the worship experience of 1 Corinthians 14:24–25, as non-Christians 'fall down' and confess, 'God is really among you!'

## Worship is gracious

Worship is not simply what happens within the diversity of the congregation, but primarily what happens between the congregation and God. The sole justification of worship lies here. Indeed, without God's presence 'in the midst', worship is an empty, meaningless parody.

Worship therefore is wholly dependent on God in his grace making himself available to his people. It rests on the veracity of God, in his faithfulness to his promises that 'if you seek him, he will be found by you' (1 Chr. 28:9; cf. 2 Chr. 15:2; Matt. 7:7), and that 'where two or three come together in my name, there am I with them' (Matt. 18:20).

Worship therefore should be 'inclusive' in the sense of allowing God himself to be a vital participant, through using a form that is consciously dialogical. Thus worship properly begins with a scriptural 'call to worship', establishing the priority of God and his invitation to 'draw near' to him. It will necessarily include moments of thanksgiving and sheer adoration, as we are moved beyond our personal

concerns to magnify him for all that he is, has done, is doing and will
do. The appropriate use of words of Scripture throughout a service,
and the sermon as an exposition of a portion of the Word of God,
further allow this critical dialogue to develop under the presidency of
God 'in the midst'.

### Jesus our fellow-worshipper!

But the gracious character of worship is further expressed as we
recognize the role of Jesus Christ in worship. Too often his role is
confined to his being the one to whom the worship is directed. The
Lord Jesus is, of course, a proper object of worship, within the
Godhead, adored and loved with all our hearts and minds. But he
also contributes at a further crucial level. We recall that during his
incarnate ministry Jesus himself participated in worship, in both
synagogue and Temple (Mark 1:39; Luke 4:16; 6:6; 22:15; John 2:13).
His was a perfect worship, part of the response he offered to God
in our humanity, on our behalf (Heb. 5:7), and now a part of his
continuing high-priestly intercession for us in the presence of the
Father (Rom. 8:34; Heb. 2:5–18; 4:14 – 5:10; 7:11–28; 9:11–28; 10:19–25).

Thus our Lord Jesus Christ is not only God the Son to whom we
direct worship, but, as God incarnate, also our fellow worshipper,
who offers a perfect human worship on our behalf as part of that
entire obedience and righteousness which is credited to us in our
justification (1 Cor. 1:30; Rom. 3:21–24; 5:1; Heb. 5:1–10; 7:23–26).

This amazing truth is wonderfully freeing, as it lifts from us the
otherwise frustrating experience of constantly offering worship that is
less than fully adequate. The truth is that as sinners we all struggle, for
much of the time in our worship, with unbelief and a less than wholehearted devotion. But Jesus, our great High Priest, clothed in our
humanity, offers in the presence of Godhead a perfect, believing and
wholehearted offering of praise.

> Jesus comes as our brother to be our great high priest, to carry on his
> heart the joys, the sorrows, the prayers, the conflicts of all his creatures
> . . . and to intercede for all nations as our eternal mediator and advocate.
> He comes to stand in for us in the presence of the Father, when in our
> failure and bewilderment we do not know how to pray as we ought, or
> forget to pray altogether. By his Spirit he helps us in our infirmities.[3]

This great, liberating truth is not, of course, confined to new-humanity congregations, but perhaps it has a special resonance in that context as the challenge to express a worship experience that is adequate is made the more demanding by the sheer diversity of the participants. Regularly achieving a worship experience that enables the authentic worship of a heterogeneous community takes time and patience. So again the sheer supernatural dimension of it all is to be underlined. But, thanks be to God, it *is* such. We are not left in worship to our own devices, or to the always questionable measure of our personal piety and sincerity. Rather, precisely here the divine dimension comes into special focus, as we worship in and by and with the endless, boundless grace of the triune God.

## Worship is inclusive

As we argued above, Christian worship needs to include the worship of all the elements in a congregation, and no-one should be disenfranchised.

### Convergent worship

Thus, in addressing issues such as the style of music to be employed or whether the vocal praise should use hymns or more recently composed songs, the answer is clearly *both*. 'Blended' is a term that has been used to denote that welcome inclusiveness. However, in order to escape the impression of a mere compromise to keep everyone happy, the term 'convergent' has more recently been coined.[4] This term recognizes the need for diversity, and hence for both the old and the new, but it also points a way to worship that positively incorporates a variety of forms, which will use Scripture in a helpful way, and which in addition, as appropriate, will use some of the traditional material from the Christian centuries, such as ancient prayers and liturgical forms.

One of the benefits of embracing the richness of biblical material in worship is that it permits a width and inclusiveness also in the variety of experience that we are able to bring to God in the course of our worship. The Psalms are a special gift at this point, reflecting as they do the whole range of human experience, from the highest moments of praise (Pss. 8; 23; 42; 84; 92 – 103; etc.) to deep, dark valleys of despair (Pss. 22; 77; 88; etc.).

### And the children

Another expression of inclusiveness is recognizing the worship ministry of young people and children. Scripture clearly affirms the reality of child faith (cf. 1 Sam. 3:1–21). No-one who has worked with children, or who has children in their home, will question the possibility of those of very early age expressing a sincere and meaningful response to God. If a congregation is committed to a worship experience that includes *all* its elements, then some place needs to be found for child-response. How this is expressed is beyond this book's parameters; however, the principle needs to be established. Children, and young people generally, are not there in worship simply to receive yet another piece of instruction. They also need to contribute periodically from their experience of the Lord, as Jesus noted (Matt. 18:1–6; 19:13–15; 21:15), and the congregation will be enriched by that giving, and will be correspondingly less than complete without it.

### Shared leadership

Still another expression of inclusiveness is the involvement of a variety of public participants in the worship experience. 1 Corinthians 14:26 clearly assumes such to be the norm, certainly in the Corinthian situation. During my years in Vancouver, we tried to ensure that all the major sub-sets of the congregation played at least some part in the public leadership over a number of weeks. It was helpful, we also found, that those so participating were part of a visible 'platform group' through, at very least, the early part of a service. The effect of this multiple participation, both verbal and visual, was that, since all the sub-groups instinctively identified with their 'representative', a general sense of ownership of the entire experience was achieved, which in turn significantly helped the overall sense of community and mutual commitment.

### All saints and angels

But, as Christians, every time we meet for worship we are part of a much larger whole. This is true at two levels. The first is that of 'all those everywhere who call on the name of our Lord Jesus Christ' (1 Cor. 1:2) – the global church. We captured this in the Introduction, in the 'worship wave'. New-humanity congregations have no greater claim on this than any others. However, when a congregation has consciously embraced ethnic diversity, in particular, this sense of global family is afforded a richer relevance.

The second dimension of the larger whole, identified earlier in Hebrews 12, is one that is often overlooked: the communion between the church militant and the church triumphant – the inclusion in our worship of 'thousands upon thousands of angels' and 'the spirits of the righteous made perfect' (cf. Heb. 12:22–23). Church furnishing can help us here with a judicious use of banners, as well as occasional reminders from those teaching Scripture from the pulpit, or leading in prayers and liturgical responses.

*Overspill*

One final point of inclusiveness to be noted is the embrace of the congregants' lives beyond the sanctuary, in home, marketplace and community. Worship in this sense needs to spill over beyond Sundays into our Monday-to-Saturday worlds. Indeed, with today's workplace revolution, it is increasingly difficult to tie down the 'working' part of many people's lives to any specific place or time. For mothers and homemakers, of course, that has always been the case. Worship needs to embrace all of life to enable Colossians 3:17, 23–24, to be honoured: 'Whatever you do, whether in word or deed, do it all in the name of the Lord Jesus, giving thanks to the Father through him . . . Whatever you do, work at it with all your heart, as working for the Lord, not for human masters . . . It is the Lord Christ you are serving.' In this respect the worship on Sunday is to be understood as the springboard for the worship to be offered through all the remaining days of the week.

Inclusiveness here will also encompass a vital interest in and concern for the world around us, its needy multitudes, its material and spiritual struggles, its political security and the pursuit of justice, as well as the stewardship of our natural environment. All these and other concerns can be woven into the texture of our approach to God as his intercessors, bringing the world to God, and then, as his servants, going into the world in his name.

*Bringing the world to God*

The concern to allow worship to spill over beyond the sanctuary implies a place in worship for authentic intercession. The loss of this in many churches today is a matter of deep concern. The explanation offered, in at least some cases, is the 'seekers after Christ' who may be in the service could be offended by an activity in which they cannot participate. In 1 Corinthians 14:24–25, however, Paul teaches that it is precisely the 'strange', spiritual, supernatural elements in a worship service that God can use to speak to non-Christians – a truth I have seen vindicated again and again over the years, not least with 'seekers' from right outside a Christian tradition. Nor can we ignore the summons of Jesus to pray, 'Your kingdom come, your will be done on earth' (Matt. 6:10), or that of 1 Timothy 2:1–2, where Paul, in issuing instructions for the conduct of public worship, makes Christian prayers for the non-Christian order, particular its political life and its leadership, a mandatory requirement (cf. also Rom. 13:4–7; 1 Pet. 2:17: Rev. 5:8; 8:3–4).

Quite apart from its biblical weakness, this vetoing of intercession appears to fail also at the level of the imagination. As a non-Christian visiting a Christian service, I would be bound to assume that these people are in touch with an almighty, sovereign God, and hence able to petition him for anything that it is appropriate to ask for. All around me I see a world dying from wars, famines, diseases like HIV/Aids, appalling poverty, injustice, the denial of basic human rights, the abuse of women and children, and environmental pollution, as well as particular people in my own life who are hurting very badly indeed. If, when in the presence of their all-powerful God, these Christians do not bring these kinds of need to him for his help and intervention, what kind of a God must he be? Is he impotent to intervene? Or does he not care? Or do *they* not care? If I were a non-Christian visiting such a church, at that point I would mentally, and then later physically, head for the door.

But, positively, intercession for the world and for the community immediately around us is a wonderful way of engaging in the depths of worship as we identify with the yearning, beating heart of God for the world in its spiritual and material needs.

A new-humanity congregation, which is committed to the local community and reflective of its peoples, will delight in intercessory prayer for the needs all around them, simply because these needs are not just ideas in the head, or even momentary images on a television screen, but real, hurting people and real, known situations needing resolution and healing.

All these dimensions of inclusiveness help in significant ways to forge the congregational identity, and to further the combining of the diversities of a new-humanity community into a richer and deeper unity.

## Worship is celebrative

Under this final heading, we of course embrace all forms and occasions of Christian worship. However, again the new-humanity model offers promise of an especially rich expression.

Christian worship occurs, commonly, on Sunday, the 'Lord's day' (Rev. 1:10), the day on which Jesus rose from the dead (Matt. 28:1; Mark 16:9). Accordingly, each weekly act of worship is a conscious reminder of the glorious fact at the heart of our faith, that on that day two thousand years ago, Jesus cleaved history asunder, triumphing over our age-long enemies, sin and evil, Satan, death and hell. 'Christ is risen. Hallelujah!'

### The ultimate defiance

Celebration is therefore a necessary note in every Christian weekly worship service. Not that the world around us is presently ready to join this Sunday jubilation. In fact, its mood is commonly precisely the antithesis of Easter joy. From this point of view, therefore, Christian worship is an act of defiance. It is the daring assertion, in the midst of a lost, divided, unbelieving and disordered world, that, despite appearances to the contrary, evil has been defeated and forfeited its dream of conquest. Sin does not have the last word, nor will death, the 'final enemy'. Christ has conquered, that is, God in Christ. His eternal kingdom has dawned and is moving on to its glorious fulfilment at the return of the Lord and the manifestation of the eternal order of righteousness, peace and joy.

All this is to be anticipated in our weekly worship experience, and in a new-humanity congregation this has special resonance as we are afforded, in the actual configuration of the congregation, a visible, tangible foretaste of that amazing multi-faceted, multi-coloured, celebrative diversity which will characterize the new order:

> Then I heard what sounded like a great multitude ... shouting:

> 'Hallelujah!
>  For our Lord God Almighty reigns.
> Let us rejoice and be glad
>  and give him glory!'
> (Rev. 19:6–7)

## LEADERSHIP

There can be few hotter topics today in industry, business, politics and community life than leadership. In such an atmosphere there is a huge temptation for Christian thinking to become conformed to the world by uncritically embracing the 'secret' of successful leadership in these secular spheres. Only too easily we forget the distinctive pattern of leadership Jesus both embodied and taught, one calling for the conscious rejection of all self-promotion and assertive domination (Matt. 23:1–12, 25–28; Luke 22:24–27; John 13:2–17), the recognition of leadership as a form of service (Luke 22:26), and a willingness on the part of leaders to sacrifice themselves (Matt. 20:28; Mark 8:34–35; 10:43, 45; Luke 14:7–11, 27; 22:42; John 13:7, 15).

Granted these perennial qualities of Christian leadership, what particular nuances arise for the practice of leadership in new-humanity congregations? In essence, the style of leadership to be sought is one that embodies Jesus' values and thereby promotes a spirit of unity throughout, and commitment to, the highly diverse body that is the new-humanity church.

### Leadership must be spiritual

As we have stated repeatedly, the achieving of authentic community from the many strands and diversities of the congregation is super-natural: it is God's work that unites his people, imparting to them the gift of the one Holy Spirit. This is true of every local church. In a new-humanity church the challenges are likely to be greater, simply because of the commitment to diversity. But the Holy Spirit indwells each member so that they form a single life-system, the body of Christ. 'We were all baptised by one Spirit into one body' (1 Cor. 12:13).

### It's a ministry...

God is the only explanation for the formation of a church; hence church leadership is necessarily a God-based, God-directed function. Accordingly, its issues are to be addressed in a spirit of prayer, waiting upon God for his help and direction. Those appointed to leadership must be persons for whom prayer, openness to God and a commitment to walking daily with God are all evident qualities. A godly society needs a godly leadership.

This Godward orientation is also expressed as the leaders solicit and receive the regular prayers of the congregation (Heb. 13:18; Eph. 6:19–20; Col. 4:3–4). Matters of special significance and difficulty need to be laid before God with particular intentionality. Time will often be set aside to wait upon God in the course of resolving them.

In turn, those who exercise leadership have a right to the respect and spiritual encouragement of the congregation (Gal. 6:6; 1 Thess. 5:12–13).

### ... before the Lord

When the whole congregation gathers to consider matters affecting their life together, God's presence will be made explicit by an atmosphere of worship, some hearing of his Word, and perhaps also the administration of the Lord's Supper. Historically, in many 'independent' church traditions, such congregational meetings would commonly have included worship, testimonies and prayer for congregational needs, as well as a eucharistic celebration. The common modern title of 'business meeting' (the preferable older title was 'church meeting' or 'congregational meeting') is an unhappy concession to secular perspectives, and can foster an unhelpful, unbiblical distinction between the 'spiritual' and the 'practical' aspects of a congregation's life.

I am reminded of a church where the earlier perspective had been recovered, so that the 'business meeting' had become a place of warmth, genuine friendship, spiritual ministry and sheer fun. A woman was heard to remark on the way out: 'That was so good, they should charge us for admission!'

## Leadership must be credible

The cardinal value of new-humanity congregations is the development of deep mutual commitment across all the diversities of its membership. How the church is led will be a major means to this. Since the way a church is led should, and over time inevitably will, reflect the way a church lives, the credibility of the leadership is the degree to which it promotes this mutual commitment. We shall note a number of ways of achieving this sense of belonging together.

Specifically, as we noted earlier, a congregation open to new-humanity principles will form other peer-identity groups, such as youth, women, men, young marrieds, and seniors. It is important that these groups be, as far as possible, represented in the leadership of the congregation. While the desire to achieve this can be carried to a point at which other important criteria of leadership are overlooked, this remains an important general goal.

### Power-sharing

One of the most challenging issues for any social group, churches included, is how power is handled. 'Organization entails the administration of power, which constantly reveals itself to be a seductive force trying to distort the gospel.'[5]

In many ways, the real test of inclusiveness for any group is its willingness to share power. When power is evidently passed to those who otherwise might have been excluded, a very important stage in a congregation's maturity has been reached. Thus, when a church that has been traditionally led by those drawn from the dominant racial group in the community begins to welcome those of other racial groups, the real test of their inclusion is a willingness to appoint members of these minority ethnicities to leadership positions.

In a church known to me, there was a recognition that a particular ethnic sub-community, which had become very significant through immigration, needed to be included in the leadership – probably, it was thought, by an appointment to one of the pastoral-associate positions when one became available. The next opening, however, occurred at the senior-associate level. After some hesitation, a qualified representative of the immigrant community was appointed to that position of considerable influence. The effect was dramatic. The numbers of that sub-community in the worship and life of the congregation exploded from the Sunday of his installation. They had been trusted with power; now they *really* knew that they were welcome. Community, to a new degree, had been achieved.

The same is true of trusting younger people. Obviously, maturity is an important biblical quality in leaders; the very term 'elders' expresses that. But young people also need to be affirmed as having gifts to contribute to a congregation's life and direction. In Vancouver we made it a custom to appoint two 'youth deacons' to our deacons' leadership group, and also to ensure that at least one younger person, and commonly two, served on all the major committees of the church, including the committee to call a new pastor. The fact that there were twenty deacons meant that the youth were never in danger of taking the congregation in an unwise direction, but their being listened to, and being trusted with power, sent a salutary signal of their inclusion, and went a long way to reducing the potential for generational wars in the congregation.

A similar inclusiveness needs to be expressed in bringing newer members into positions of leadership. At times congregations can be so slow/reluctant to do this that newcomers feel shut out, and eventually signal their unhappiness by finding another church home where they can use their gifts. Obviously a balance needs to be maintained here, but taking risks by including people will more often reap dividends than engender problems.

Nor dare we forget the continuing contribution of older people. Older Christian disciples are sometimes given the message by their church that their days of significant contribution are now entirely over, duplicating the message signalled in the surrounding society when they reach retirement. But again we need to take our values from Scripture, not the culture. I think of Christine, a lady in her nineties with a life of service in a professional nursing agency, who was called into a consultation on the future of the agency in recognition of the value of her perspective. It is sad when the church fails to rise to the level of the secular community in harnessing the experience of its oldest members.

*Danger points*

We need to be alert to the dangers inherent when leadership becomes too firmly rooted in a particular sub-group. Sometimes, this arises in smaller congregations with the added undergirding of family bonds.

A recent report of a conversation between a major missions agency in South Africa and a group of congregations in a particular area carried this sub-heading: 'DON'T build homogeneous churches again! Especially if the family is the basis of the unity' (their capitals). In this instance, mission work had been conducted with the aim of establishing different church groups among different ethnic sectors of the population. The result was the tragedy of congregations with inbuilt family solidarities that were now barriers to growth and credibility in their communities. One of the participants in the conversation spoke of a case where family members lined up behind a leader who was evidently morally in the wrong, simply because of family loyalty rather than loyalty to the family of God. Who could not replicate that from Western experience?

Another danger is when the leadership becomes confined to one social group. Michael Moynagh notes the experience of a church in a poor area of south-east England:

> It was making great strides in attracting people from the immediate community. It became seen as a successful church, and so middle-class Christians from further afield began to attend. After a couple of years, the original, working-class members started to leave. 'It doesn't feel the same any more,' they complained. Unintentionally, the new arrivals had changed the culture, made it a little more 'bookish', and the less well-educated felt no longer at home.[6]

## Leadership must be accountable

Another critical way to promote new-humanity community is to ensure that the leadership not only arises from the whole body of a congregation but should be continually in relationship to it. Certain matters will call for confidentiality, but these should be kept to a minimum and ways should be found of making the process as transparent and accountable as possible.

It is important in this regard that those in leadership should express a true caring spirit as far as the congregation is concerned. The prayer life of the leaders, which we noted earlier, should include regular intercession for the membership as a whole, and leaders need to be actively involved with the congregations they lead. No delegation of leadership to a specific ministry area (e.g. 'leader of youth' or 'leader of administration') should be taken as a directive to confine oneself in one's concern and prayers to that area of the church's life. It is arguably better to be less than fully abreast of one's own area of responsibility than to be quite unaware of the concerns and life-situation of the wider congregation.

### For all the people

Accordingly, leaders need to be, and to be seen to be, persons who exhibit a true love of their fellow members and are willing to spend time with them and relate to them. All ministry is finally people-ministry, and a loving, caring spirit in the leadership will always percolate down to the members. Nowhere is this more critical than in the chief pastoral leader, but it is relevant right across the board in the ministry style of the leaders generally. The converse is, of course, equally and sadly true. Jess Moody captures this staple of ministry and leadership in a memorable sentence: 'People don't go where the action is; they go where the love is.'[7] Loving leaders produce, with time, loving congregations. And loving congregations draw people, and hold those they draw.

Richard Baxter's seventeenth-century call to the pastoral leaders of his day could not be improved on for all in leadership today and tomorrow:

All the flock, even each individual member of our charge, must be taken heed of and watched over by us in our ministry. To which end it is necessary that we should know every person that belongs to our charge. For how can we take heed of them if we do not know them? We must labour to be acquainted with the state of all our people as fully as we can, with their inclinations and conversations; to know what are the sins they are most in danger of, and what duties they neglect and what temptations they are most liable to. For if we know not their temperament or disease we are likely to prove but unsuccessful physicians ... The whole course of our ministry must be carried on in tender love of our people ... Yea, the tenderest love of a mother should not surpass ours.[8]

But how do we develop this 'mother love'? One of its keys lies in the final aspect to be noted.

## Leadership must be vulnerable

One of the continual dangers of leadership is the trap of imagining that our role as leaders sets us above those we lead, in the sense of rendering us impervious to their weaknesses, temptations and struggles; or, at least, that it requires us to act as if that were the case.

It therefore comes as something of a shock to realize from Scripture that God's leaders have been consistently weak people, who have known failure in their lives. It is Noah, caught in the improprieties associated with his drunkenness, whom God chooses to lead humanity through the flood (Gen. 9:20–23). It is Abraham, who in his fear tells lies about his wife, whom God chooses to lead his people into the covenant of redemption (Gen. 12:10–20). It is Joseph, the eleventh son of Jacob, the one who provokes his brothers with his flaunting pride, who becomes the leader of Egypt and the means of the preservation of God's people (Gen. 37:1–11). It is Moses, a murderer, who is called to lead Israel out of the Egyptian enslavement and to see God's mighty works at the Red Sea (Exod. 2:11–14). It is Rahab, a prostitute, who becomes the instrument of God's plan of annexation (Josh. 2:1–14). In the New Testament, it is Peter, who publicly denied his Lord three times, who is the first great leader of the church (Matt. 26:69–75). It is Paul, a former 'blasphemer, persecutor and violent man', who is the leader of the mission to the Gentiles, and the composer, through the Holy Spirit, of a larger part of the New Testament than any other contributor (1 Tim. 1:13).

This list is not, of course, intended to contradict the clear insistence in Scripture on the need for godliness in those who are called to leadership.[9] However, it is a salutary reminder that our attainment of such is always 'on the way' in this life, in the case of leaders as well as those who follow them.

### Perfected in weakness

Paul's lesson with respect to his 'thorn' (2 Cor. 12:7–10) is essential study for every Christian leader, whatever their level of responsibility. God, to our great surprise, is attracted, not to strength, but to weakness. His divine strength is perfected through it. It is a continual recognizing of our deep vulnerability and utter dependence that keeps us close to him. But also, amazingly, it is that same spirit of dependence, even helplessness, that will keep us close also to those we are called to lead.

Sheila Cassidy, writing out of her experience of hospice ministry to the dying, writes:

> More than anything else I have learned that we are all frail people, vulnerable and wounded; it is just that some of us are cleverer at concealing it than others ... The world is not divided into the strong who care, and the weak who are cared for. We must each in turn care and be cared for, not just because it is good for us, but because that is the way things are. The hardest thing for those of us who are professional carers is to admit that we are in need, peel off our sweaty socks and let someone else wash our dirty, blistered feet.[10]

A humble spirit, a walk with God characterized by a conscious, daily dependence on his grace, a sensitivity to our own limitations and regular shortcomings – such is the leadership style that will in time produce a congregation where the 'weary and burdened' from all the parameters of diversity will be drawn together in the 'rest' provided by him who is 'gentle and humble in heart' (Matt. 11:28–30).

The responsibilities of leadership are very real, and at times very heavy. But what a privilege also lies here, and what a means of bringing honour and glory to God! To develop and shape a congregation whose caring and compassionate heart reaches out to the needy, represented not least by those who are different from ourselves in all kinds of ways, is a supreme privilege indeed. And it leads to many others, as those who have been drawn to Christ look to us to afford them further encouragement and support as they grow in their knowledge and service of God.

## 8 Down to earth

*Discipleship and fellowship in the new-humanity church*

Worship and leadership focus the primary shared activity and the essential structures of a congregation's life. In this chapter we shall consider new-humanity perspectives in the further significant areas of the congregation's growth through discipleship, and its mutual relationships expressed in fellowship.

### DISCIPLESHIP

The promotion of discipleship is a primary responsibility of every church: 'teaching them to obey all that I have commanded you' (Matt. 28:19; cf. Acts 2:42; 2 Cor. 10:15; Eph. 4:15; Col. 1:10; 2:19; 2 Thess. 1:3; Heb. 6:1; 1 Pet. 2:2; 2 Pet. 3:18). It includes all the means employed to foster Christian growth.

The following section attempts to summarize the primary 'promoters of growth' and to note particular nuances for a congregation modelling itself on new-humanity principles.

## A Bible-directed lifestyle

God's supreme means of renewing and growing his people is his Word, the written Scriptures (John 17:17; 2 Tim. 3:16). Hence we note the centrality of the teaching of the Word in the work of pastoral leaders (2 Tim. 4:2; cf. also 1 Tim. 3:2; 4:11, 13; 5:17; 2 Tim. 2:15, 25; Titus 1:9; 2:1–9, 15). Paul is a great model in this (Acts 20:20–21, 32). Just as God the Holy Spirit uses Scripture in bringing people to faith in Christ (Eph. 1:13), so he continues to use it in conforming them to Christ (Eph. 5:26–27).

Personal, private study of Scripture with a view to understanding its teaching and embodying it in our lives is essential if we are serious in our discipleship. We are challenged in this regard by the Bereans, who 'examined the Scriptures every day' (Acts 17:11). Disciples follow Jesus, and we hear his voice and meet him, the incarnate Word, in the written Word (John 5:39). The teaching of the Word of God in the context of worship is a further fundamental means of Christian growth. Virtually all the biblical references to growing through the Scriptures we have cited in the last paragraphs are to our exposure to the Word of God in that context.

### Written Word, incarnate Word

One of the obvious ways in which Scripture is central in the process of discipleship is that it maps out the goal to which all our discipleship is directed. In sum, this is nothing less than our conformity to Christ (1 John 3:2; 2 Cor. 3:18). However, the Bible not only unveils the astonishing climax to our journey as learners with Jesus; it also spells out in considerable detail what this 'likeness to Christ' looks like here and now.

The letter to the Ephesians is a good example. Here is a statement of the goal: 'attaining to the whole measure of the fulness of Christ' (4:13), becoming 'like God in true righteousness and holiness' (4:24). But here, too, are specific features of this Christ-likeness, this conformity to God.

Six marks are identified:

- Unity: 4:2–16
- Truth: 4:25–30

- Love: 4:31 – 5:2
- Purity: 5:3–14
- Wisdom: 5:15–17
- Praise: 5:18–21

The spelling-out of the terms of godliness is important because a new-humanity instinct for inclusion needs to be attuned to these specific values, and hence to the God-honouring goals of being godly as well as generous, righteous as well as receptive, disciplined as well as diverse, holy as well as whole.

These biblical markers of the God-honouring community lifestyle make it clear that new-humanity inclusiveness is not morally indiscriminate. This is not least the case in the sphere of sexual mores, as Ephesians 5:3–14 underlines. A specific clarification is required here, as the adjective 'inclusive' has come to mean, for some, a tolerance of sexual partnerships, particularly homosexual ones, that contravene the biblical mandate in Genesis 2:24, which sets genital sexual relationships firmly within monogamous heterosexual marriage. Anything beyond that, whether heterosexual or homosexual, falls under Paul's censure in Ephesians 5:3, as well as the censure of Jesus, implicit in his endorsement of the Genesis 2:24 pronouncement in Matthew 19:4.

The issue of gay lifestyles and relationships is a highly charged one at the present time, and has already caused division both in churches and in wider society. Christians are, however, without exception, called to faithfulness to the clear teaching of Scripture, not least in this area.

Faithfulness is of course also required in fulfilling the command to love our neighbour as ourselves (Mat. 22:37–40; cf. Eph. 4:31 – 5:2), not forgetting Jesus' clarification of the scope of 'neighbour' (Luke 10:25–37). It includes all persons we encounter in our daily lives, in any degree of need, not least those towards whom we might be inclined to hold negative attitudes.[1]

Scripture calls us to offer all areas of our lives to God in obedience, with a view to our becoming more conformed to him. Although the goal of this is his glory, the blessings of it are ours, as Murray McCheyne noted: 'There is no joy like the joy of holiness.'[2]

## The Word of God in preaching

The study of Scripture as a primary means to making progress in our conformity to Christ also involves our hearing it expounded in the context of public worship. What are the 'preaching values' most likely to promote new-humanity community?

### Preaching must be biblical

As we noted, nothing is so conducive of our growth in Christ than the Word of God. Since that growth is horizontal with our neighbour, as well as vertical with our God, the ministry of the Word in preaching becomes a critical means of developing new-humanity diversity in unity.

The sermon should set out to expound Scripture. The Greek term that defines such preaching is *ektithēmi* (Acts 11:4; 28:23). The essential meaning is illustrated vividly in Acts 7:21, where baby Moses, after being raised for three months 'in his father's house', was 'placed outside'. In other words, he was put out in the open, exposed to public view; he was 'expounded'. So in biblical preaching the Word of God is to be 'brought out into the open' by being publicly stated and clarified so that its meaning and message can be heard, understood and responded to.

Three significant benefits accrue from such preaching.

Firstly, *it is authoritative*. It carries behind it the supreme authority of the words of the living God. No-one who has used this method and tasted its humbling and yet exhilarating sense of divine authority would readily resort to any other.

Secondly, *it is empowering*. God the Holy Spirit uses the Word of God. When Scripture is laid bare, and then sensitively applied, things happen. People are changed; attitudes are altered; faith is engendered and deepened; hope is born; new energies are released; characters are shaped; lives are sanctified. The psalmist calls it a lamp to our feet and a light for our path (Ps. 119:105); Peter calls it milk (1 Pet. 2:2); the writer to the Hebrews speaks of it as sharper than a sword (Heb. 4:12). Jesus sees it as the means to our being set apart for God (John 17:17), and Paul comprehensively sees it as a source of teaching, rebuking, correcting and training in righteousness, enabling men and women to be 'thoroughly equipped for every good work' (2 Tim. 3:16).

Thirdly, *it makes the Bible accessible*. Many congregations today, all over the world, are in relative ignorance of Scripture. An expository method addresses that ignorance and allows new confidence in handling Scripture. Hence, as happened in the sixteenth century when the Reformation put the Bible back in the hands of the laity, the Bible again becomes a book for all the people of God.

### Preaching must be pastoral

To develop the pastoral analogy, the sheep need to have the food prepared for them in a form that they can readily consume. Good shepherds, of whom Jesus was the Chief (1 Pet. 5:4), lead the sheep to where they will 'find pasture' (John 10:9). The challenge here is never-ending. But the aim is clear: 'exposition with application'.

It goes without saying that preachers need also to be pastors who know their sheep, like Jesus (John 10:14). Again, the ideal is always higher than the attainment, but the attempt must be made. It is in knowing the congregation, their struggles and fears, their doubts and temptations, their dreams and longings, their sins and shortcomings, their often astonishing courage and achievements, their everyday lives and special characteristics, that the preaching is informed and comes alive, and all kinds of meaningful, sensitive applications of the biblical text are evoked. Such diligent pastoral work is the irreplaceable hinterland of effective congregational preaching. In this light, the growing habit in some churches of dividing congregational responsibilities between a 'preaching minister' and a 'pastoral minister' can be viewed only with deep regret. In a new-humanity church, where the quality of the communal life and its overall relationship to God are primary concerns, such a division is unthinkable.

### Preaching must be inclusive

A new-humanity congregation sets out intentionally to bridge the various divisions within the surrounding culture. Preaching in such a setting therefore faces the challenge of being relevant to a wide diversity of human contexts.

I found great value, when ministering weekly in such a congregational setting, in developing what might be loosely termed 'scatter-preaching'. This required departing from the widely held homiletical principle that the sermon should build itself around a single point or a single theme. Rather, as the chosen Bible passage was examined, an intentional search was made for a number of distinct points of application, which, owing to the inexhaustible resource of Holy Scripture, would almost inevitably rise to the surface. Then the sub-points of the sermon regularly became a series of different applications.

Thomas Long has similar counsel: 'Sermons should be faithful to the full range of a text's power, and those preachers who carry away only the main idea are traveling too light.'[2]

This method is actually not particularly modern. Puritan preaching would commonly, in its concluding portion, identify a series of diverse 'uses' of the biblical text that had been expounded in the earlier part of the sermon.

### Scattering the seed

The adoption of this method enables a 'scattering' of the Word (an image with a rather good pedigree; Matt. 13:3, 18–23, 24, 37). In my experience, most congregants do not require to be gripped by the lapels in the first words of a sermon, and held in that grip right through to its final sentence, in order to hear God speak through it, and hence to want to come the following week to listen again. Rather, provided that *at some point in the message* they hear what represents for them the living God speaking livingly into their hearts and lives, they will recognize God's presence in the Word, and be eager to hear it again the following Sunday.

A significant practical, methodological aid in achieving this 'scatter-ing' in application is to ask of the sermon, as it comes towards its final form: 'What does this message have in it for our young people? For our seniors? For our business people? For our homemakers? For the despairing? For the tempted? For the comfortable? For the fearful? For the seeker? For the one who has lost the way? For the doubting?', and so on.

For new-humanity preaching, this style is a natural fit for the diversity in the congregation being addressed. Of similar value in enabling a diversity of truth and its application is preaching system-atically through a wide range of sections of the Bible in Old and New Testaments. And, of course, one dare not forget in all of this the ministry of the Holy Spirit, who again and again totally surprises us by the way he uses Scripture and applies it, in all kinds of ways and at all kinds of points, of which we are entirely ignorant. I frequently had the (delightful) surprise, shared by all preachers, of being pointedly thanked for a particular sermon, or a particular point in its application, by a member of the congregation for whom I had real anxiety as to whether there would have been anything for them in the message that Sunday. God uses his Word to disciple his people.

### Preaching must be face-to-face
In a congregation where the development of human community is a priority, careful and prayerful thought is critical with respect to the forms of communication employed, week by week, in its primary shaping event, the worship service. This applies to how the worship is led, the music, the points and forms of congregational involvement, the style of verbal communication and so on. A similar and perhaps even greater degree of care needs to be given to the form of communication employed in what is arguably the primary shaping event, the pastor-to-people relationship expressed in the sermon.

At this point respect needs to be accorded to studies that have consistently shown that the most human, personal and hence community-building form of communication, for all human generations and types, is aurality, direct speech, face-to-face and person-to-person.[3]

Accordingly, we must carefully weigh the question of whether modern communications forms, which intrude into, or to a real degree reduce, face-to-face, person-to-person communication, are to be encouraged – however 'cool', 'postmodern' and generationally comfortable for some congregants. Apart from the theological questions raised here concerning the form of God's communication with us in his incarnate, personal Word, modern visual communication tools, when employed as the accompaniment of preaching in congregational worship settings, also carry major liabilities for those intent on developing 'high-touch', new-humanity congregations.

Firstly, they threaten one of the charter principles of such congregations: they cater to one or two generations at the expense of the others. Aurality, by contrast, is a communication form that is accessible to, and meaningful for, all generations.

Secondly, they can in effect insert a filter between the congregation and the preacher, and accordingly inhibit the direct and personal quality of the communication. The danger clearly exists of being at the cutting-edge point for communication while being simultaneously at the cutting-off point for community.

### Legislators and lawyers

It is to the point, in this connection, that a recognition of the unique authority and personal quality of direct, aural communication informs the global worlds of government and jurisprudence. In every parliament on earth, legislation is defended, criticized and enacted on the basis of aural, face-to-face communication, through personally delivered speeches. In every courtroom in the world, justice is established through the verbal arguments and counter-arguments of advocates, and the direct, verbal, face-to-face interrogation of witnesses. In the awesome calling to speak for God as his heralds, ought we to resort to forms that are less direct and less personal than that recognized as uniquely appropriate for supremely serious communication by the secular world?

It has to be conceded that direct aural communication may itself also fail in respect of its personal quality and community-building potential. Excessive immersion in written notes delivered in a cold, impersonal lecture style will obviously also inhibit preacher-to-people communication, as will language that is over the heads, or remote from the experience, of the listeners.

More generally, preaching, to be effective, needs to accept, even embrace, its inherent and incurable weakness – not, of course, the weakness of shoddy preparation or careless presentation, but the weakness born of the fact that, soberly considered, preaching is impossible! How can *any* human speak for God? But that weakness is also its supreme glory and strength, for it casts the preacher back utterly upon God and the ministry of his gracious, powerful Spirit. Hence, not being a 'strong' or 'cool' communicator is not necessarily a liability, but can in fact be a part of our preaching's secret power.[4]

The principles underlying this section do need, at very least, to be carefully weighed. If we are concerned to produce rich levels of community, then *how* we communicate at all points in the weekly worship service, and not least in the sermon, becomes a matter of considerable significance. The relationships within a congregation, much more than we commonly imagine, reflect the leaders' interaction among themselves, the form and quality of the leaders' communication with the congregation at large, and the ways in which all of that is expressed in the congregation's primary formative experience week by week, the worship service.

## Small groups

Subdividing a congregation into small groups, commonly of around a dozen members or affiliates, for purposes of fellowship, mutual support, prayer and Bible study or discussion, is a widespread practice in our time. New-humanity congregations, with their high priority on mutuality across diversities, are likely to be drawn to this form more than most. The stratifying of the membership so that the diversity of the congregation is reflected in the composition of the groups is an important goal.

Small groups do have dangers. They can become a platform on which stronger or more knowledgeable members too frequently display their superior capacities. Small groups can encourage an unhealthy, prying spirit if the members commit to sharing their deeper feelings and struggles. The groups can also develop an inappropriate loyalty which overrides loyalties to the church's leaders, or to the church as a whole; this danger is likely to be deepened if the group's membership remains unchanged for too long a period. All these dangers can be largely counteracted by good leadership.

On the other side of the ledger, however, there are significant blessings that can accrue, not least for a new-humanity fellowship.

First, *encouragement*. Hebrews 3:13, 'Encourage one another daily', says it exactly. We remember that the Holy Spirit is named as 'the Encourager' (a possible translation of John 14:16). His encouragement is regularly ministered through fellow disciples, and a small-group context is an obvious sphere for that to occur.

Second, *burden-bearing*. 'Carry each other's burdens' (Gal. 6:2); 'We who are strong ought to bear with the failings of the weak' (Rom. 15:1; cf. 1 Thess. 5:14). Provided that we do not see 'strong' and 'weak' as rigid classifications, this very aptly identifies one of the primary values of small groups. We are all at times burdened believers, needing the support of our fellow Christians. One need only reflect on the obvious point that the great bulk of the New Testament's teaching on discipleship is conveyed in letters written to churches rather than to individuals. Christian growth is essentially contemplated, not as a lonely struggle to reach a forbidding moral summit, but as a shared reality in the context of a burden-bearing community.

Paul Tournier tells of meeting his pastor one day.

'You never visit me,' said the pastor.

'Oh, you don't need it. I go and see the lost sheep.'

To which Tournier poignantly replied, 'Am I not also a lost sheep? ... I have seen Christians weeping in my counseling room, "pillars of the church" on whom everyone depended, but whom no one troubled to help in their personal difficulties.'[5]

We all need each other, and a small-group setting allows that ministry of mutual care to be expressed in a very meaningful way.

Third, *prayer*. Jesus taught his disciples to pray, 'When you pray, say, "Father, hallowed be your name..."' (Luke 11:2). He also assumed that his disciples would be people who prayed frequently: 'Jesus told his disciples a parable to show them that they should always pray and not give up' (Luke 18:1). A small group is a natural setting in which to learn how to pray for others, and to experience the special joy of prayers being answered.

Fourth, *accountability*. The idea that we are accountable to our fellow Christians within the body of Christ is a difficult one, not widely recognized today. But Jesus taught the need to be continually reconciled. 'If you are offering your gift at the altar and there remember that your brother or sister has something against you, leave your gift ... go and be reconciled to them; then come and offer your gift' (Matt. 5:23–24). Our mutual relationships are so significant that our offering to God in worship is affected by them. James even writes, 'Confess your sins to each other' (James 5:16). This needs sensitive handling, and small-group contexts may not be the best place for such. But the idea of accountability to fellow believers is clear, and a small-group setting can be an appropriate context in which to express it.

Fifth, *hospitality*. The Old Testament has many examples of this ministry (cf. Gen. 18:1–5; Exod. 2:20; Judg. 13:15; 1 Kgs 17:7–16; 2 Kgs 4:8–10). Jesus exalted the offering of hospitality as one of the ways in which he was ministered to in his 'brothers and sisters' (Matt. 25:40), for 'I was a stranger and you invited me in' (25:35). So, 'Offer hospitality to one another without grumbling', says Peter (1 Pet. 4:9;

cf. Rom. 12:13). The practice of hospitality is put high on the list of an elder/bishop's qualifications (1 Tim. 3:2; Titus 1:8). Small-group occasions are an obvious way to express that calling, though of course this is not the only occasion for its expression, recalling Jesus' association of it with ministry to the hungry, the naked, the thirsty, the sick and the prisoner (Matt. 25:34–36).

It is to be remembered that 'the home was the centre of the common life of the church during its first two hundred years'.[6] I recall a church that created a large lounge, imitating in every detail the average lounge in the homes surrounding its building, so that people coming into church for the first time immediately felt at home.

Another way of harnessing the power of the home in building community, which we tried with considerable success in Vancouver, was to have one Sunday twice a year entitled 'Guess who's coming to lunch Sunday'. On that day, hosts or hosting families cooked enough of a simple menu to provide lunch for around half a dozen people, and then the members of the congregation, after the morning services, were allocated a home for lunch. People's earlier commitment to be a part of the event, plus imaginative co-ordination, helped to create rich diversity in the lunch groups. The result was always a deepened sense of belonging together.

Yan Zhao from China speaks for a multitude:

Before I came to Christ I had very little life. Most of my time was spent either in the library or in my room. I have no family member living in this city and I had very few friends. I felt isolated from the outside world and on the edge of collapse. Life seemed hopeless for me so I began searching for help. I remembered a friend of mind invited me to her church group about a year ago ... so that Friday night I came to the International Ministry for the first time in my life. I had never attended a church before. I had no idea of what was the world inside its building. I must say that is a group of the most wonderful people I've ever met. I appreciate all their dedication, their care and love. They have made it possible for me to come to Christ ... A few months later I completed the Alpha course. I enjoyed a great deal of our group discussion. It was just wonderful. They cared about me and helped each other and me. I really felt I had found another family, and it is the church. At the end of the course I made up my mind to commit myself to Christ. Now I understand why Jesus is the direction of my life. By following his words I shall not be lost and be anxious about my future. I know I will become a better person. I want to be baptized because I want to publicly announce that I have become a Christian, and I'm a member now of the most wonderful family.

Small-group ministry is, as we have noted, a context for Christian growth that allows the expression of many important aspects of Christian discipleship. It is of special value for any congregation that sets itself to embrace diversity in its widest terms, as it offers a relaxed atmosphere in small enough numbers for deep mutual understanding and commitment to develop. If the groups can be stratified to ensure the interaction of difference, the health of relationships in the congregation as a whole stands to benefit immensely.

## One-to-one discipleship

While the benefits of small-group discipling are evident and proven over a wide variety of congregational types, it may not be sufficient in itself to meet the need, particularly if the congregation is experiencing growth through the coming to faith of people in adult years. New-humanity congregations are likelier than most to experience this form of growth.

In today's world, many grow into adulthood with the most hazy and confused understanding of what Christianity teaches, of what a Christian is and of what a Christian life involves. In such a context, while not negating the inner enlightenment of the Holy Spirit, people coming to the Lord have massive gaps in their understanding. As we discovered in Vancouver, with many postmodern, young adults coming to Christ, a small group is often not the best way to help them become established. A small-group experience may well follow later, but at the earliest stage they need something that is more adaptable to their personal needs. This first step in discipleship is a one-to-one ministry. There are some excellent biblical models: Philip with the Ethiopian eunuch (Acts 8:26–40); Barnabas with Paul (Acts 11:25); or Aquila and Priscilla's 'two-to-one' ministry to Apollos (Acts 18:26).

A syllabus covering the basics of Christian faith and practice can readily be drawn up, covering topics such as 'What is the gospel?', 'What happened when I became a Christian?', 'How can I be sure in my faith?', 'What is church about?', 'Why be committed to a church?', 'Baptism as the door in', 'What worship is, and how worship services are designed to facilitate it', 'How to pray', 'An introduction to the Bible, and how to read it daily', 'Christian values for personal relationships', 'Relating to others', 'Dealing with temptation', 'Being a witness for Christ', 'How to be a Christian in the marketplace, the home and the community', and 'Identifying my gift and how to contribute it'. The new Christian is taken through that syllabus by their more mature, trained discipler, at whatever pace is appropriate. The process continues as long as needed, whereupon the discipler becomes available to help other new 'babes in Christ' take their first steps and find some simple, basic answers to their questions.

### Inter-generational possibilities

A particularly exciting dimension of this kind of discipling is the opportunity it gives for inter-generational sharing. New-humanity churches consciously set out to include all the generations and to enable them to relate meaningfully. The Bible has so many examples of cross-generational community; Abraham with Isaac, Moses with Joshua, Samuel with David, Ruth with Naomi, Elizabeth with Mary, Peter with John, Paul with Timothy. Scripture's use of 'elders' underlines the importance of having those who have travelled further on the road of faith make their wisdom available to those who follow.

At this point a wonderfully enriching possibility emerges for older Christians in a congregation, who sadly often feel that they are no longer of particular value. They are given a new ministry for which their age and experience become their strength and gift to the church, as of course it was always intended to be. New and younger Christians are enabled to receive that wisdom shared in a warm, unthreatening context. This discipleship model is replete with the promise of rich and mutually enhancing relationships which can transcend the immediate demands of the discipleship programme and blossom into lifelong friendship.

In my mind's eye I can see Theresa, a widow and former missionary in China, her face aglow with delight. She is leading down the aisle, towards me, an about-to-be bride who had come from a very broken background to know the Lord, and whom Theresa had discipled with great love, patience and prayer over the previous two years. And that story could be replicated many times.

It is a classic 'win-win' case for the disciple and the discipler; or better, 'win-win–win-win', because the blessing is also the Lord's as his child is nurtured into a life of fruitful service, and finally the congregation's as it becomes criss-crossed with ties that make generational wars a virtual non-possibility.

## Suffering

As in the life of the Master, so in the life of a disciple community, suffering is inevitable. 'Those who would come after me must deny themselves and take up their cross and follow me' (Mark 8:34). Jesus' terms for discipleship have not changed over the centuries. 'If the world hates you, keep in mind that it hated me first ... "Servants are not greater than their masters." if they have persecuted me, they will persecute you also' (John 15:18, 20).

The range of sufferings is very wide. Job's were proverbial, involving family tragedy, deep personal losses, health breakdown, unjust accusations, financial woes, and a long struggle in the darkness of doubt due to God's seeming absence (cf. 23:10; etc.). The Psalms have similar testimonies to agonizing personal struggles (cf. Pss. 10; 13; 22; 44; 51; 55; 69; 73; 74; 77; 88). Paul can appropriately be our representative of New Testament discipleship suffering when he refers to pressures 'on every side', the perplexities of not knowing what to do or where to turn, direct persecution, and the blows (which 'struck [him] down') of dark circumstances (2 Cor. 4:8–9).

The good news of the Scriptures, however, is that God works in these and similar situations for our good. In fulfilling his purpose of conforming the church to the image of Christ, and releasing its witness more fully in the world, God uses suffering both corporate and personal. (cf. Gen. 41:52; 50:20; Ps. 119:67, 71; John 15:2; Rom. 5:3; Heb. 12:4–13; 1 Pet. 1:6–7).

Samuel Rutherford testified: 'Faith is the better of the free air, and the sharp winter storm in its face. Grace withers without adversity.'

Further, in Hudson Taylor's words, 'Difficulties afford God a platform upon which he can show himself. Without them we would never know how tender, faithful and almighty he is.'

God's plans for our lives are so much bigger than ours for ourselves. He loves us too much to leave us to our often grubby little dreams. C. S. Lewis expressed it memorably:

> Imagine yourself as a living house. God comes in to rebuild that house. At first, perhaps, you can understand what he is doing. He is getting the drains right and stopping the leaks in the roof and so on; you knew these jobs needed doing and so you are not surprised. But presently he starts knocking the house about in a way that hurts abominably and does not seem to make sense. What on earth is he up to? The explanation is that he is building quite a different house than the one you thought of – throwing out a new wing here, putting on an extra floor there, running up towers, making courtyards. You thought you were going to be made into a decent little cottage; but he is building a palace. He intends to come and live in it himself.[7]

New-humanity congregations are no different from any others in the application of these principles; however, it may be that the attempt to confront diversity and include within the congregation's embrace people who are 'different' exposes the church to additional challenges and calls for a deeper spirit of faith that the Lord is at work through such relational tensions. One of the primary New Testament values is 'perseverance' (cf. Luke 8:15; Rom. 5:3; 2 Cor. 6:4; 2 Thess. 1:4; James 1:3–4; Rev. 1:9; 3:10). It is an important grace in any church grappling to unite diversity. But the reward of such struggle is a rich and fulfilling one; our being enabled to 'grow up into him who is the Head, that is, Christ. From him the whole body, joined and held together by every supporting ligament, grows and builds itself up in love' (Eph. 4:15–16).

## FELLOWSHIP

'Fellowship' (koinōnia), which literally means 'having a share with someone in something', is one of the fundamentals of any church.[8]

Acts 2:42 reminds us that rich and meaningful fellowship was an immediate fruit of the birth of the church at Pentecost. The early chapters of Acts indicate that this vibrant sense of community energized the church right through the first period of its life (Acts 4:32–35; 5:12; 6:7; 9:31). A congregation without the experience of fellowship is a congregation in name only; like a walking corpse, it may have an appearance of life, but is in fact dead.

*Koinōnia* has been a mark of disciples of Jesus all through the centuries, and clearly provides the context within which Christian growth is intended to take place. When circumstances beyond our control dictate the loss of a supportive community, God will not desert us (1 Kgs 19:1–18; Acts 23:11), but it is here, within the body of Christ in our local church, that God typically meets us and furthers our discipleship (1 Cor. 12:24–26; Gal. 6:2; 1 Thess. 5:14).

A primary means of enriching fellowship is the meal that Jesus left us (1 Cor. 11:23–26). Variously entitled, the Lord's Supper brings the wonder of renewed communion with Jesus himself and the reaffirmation of the blessings of his covenant with us through his atoning sacrifice. 'This is my body . . . This is my blood of the covenant, which is poured out for many for the forgiveness of sins' (Matt. 26:26–28). But it also brings the renewal of our relationships with one another, our belonging together as the people of God, the one new humanity in the Spirit.

The challenge to 'keep the unity of the Spirit through the bond of peace' (Eph. 4:3) is real for every congregation.

> To live above with saints we love,
> Now that will be the glory.
> To live below with those we know,
> Ah! That's another story!

Spurgeon struck a note of realism when he remarked, 'There are religious people about whom I have no doubt that they were born of a woman, but they appear to have been suckled by a wolf'.[9] When we throw into the mix even a few of the diversities we have identified again and again through these chapters, the challenge becomes daunting indeed.

## Embracing diversity

To consider only ethnic diversity, the suburban congregation mentioned in chapter 4 (p. 76) gives a glimpse of the potential mix: a Chinese space-aeronautics engineer stuck with selling radios; an environmental professor from Colombia in exile from the work he is passionately committed to among indigenous people back home; the Iranian nominal Muslim telecommunications specialist; the French-Canadian warehouser; the Japanese exchange student, the Korean teenager, and the recently widowed long-standing Canadian resident. How do you bring that group together into a meaningful, and mutually supportive, community in Christ?

## Love is the way

We have noted the place of rites and structures that facilitate fellowship in a local church, such as the Lord's Supper and small groups. However, rites and structures can never produce fellowship between Christians unless they are accompanied by, and are productive of, a genuine attitude of concern for one another. The name for that concern is *love*. Love is the lifeblood of fellowship. Where it is present, fellowship is present, and spiritual growth will invariably occur.

Let's underline it: the kind of diversity in unity for which we are pleading is not easy to attain. We need look no further than the experience of the early church, where, despite the blessing of the outpoured Spirit at Pentecost (Acts 2), within a comparatively short time the Christians found themselves struggling to preserve the supernatural, God-given unity in a dispute over daily food distribution (Acts 6:1–7). For community to happen, love is not just helpful, it is essential.

### Grace-love

The common New Testament word for Christian love is *agapē*. Two things are to grasped about *agapē*-love. The first is that *agapē* is commonly used for the love of God revealed in the cross. John provides a definition: 'This is love [*agapē*]: not that we loved God, but that he loved [*agapasen*] us and sent his Son as an atoning sacrifice for our sins' (1 John 4:10). The special quality of the love revealed at the cross is its gracious nature; it is a love for sinners, for those who in no way deserve it (cf. Rom. 5:8, 10; Eph. 2:1–5). As against the classical culture of the first century, which commonly thought of love as in some sense earned – love for those worthy of it – Jesus expressed a love for the unworthy, *agapē*-love. This in turn is what Christians are called to express to others. 'Love [*agapate*] each other as I have loved [*ēgapēsa*] you' (John 15:12). Indeed, Jesus goes as far as to assert that this stooping, gracious love will be the distinguishing mark of his disciples: 'By this everyone will know that you are my disciples, if you love [*agapēn*] one another' (John 13:35). In the same vein is his prayer that his followers would be so united, 'one' as the Father and the Son are one, as 'to let the world know that you sent me' (John 17:23; cf. 17:21). It was precisely *agapē*-love in the lives of the first generations of Christians, as we noted in chapter 5, that made such a powerful impact on the surrounding pagan culture.

### More than a feeling

The second thing about *agapē*-love is that it is primarily an action, rather than an emotion. 'God so [*agapē*-]loved the world that he gave . . .' (John 3:16). Emotion is, of course, most commonly involved, particularly when the commitment is a deep one; but the initial movement lies in the will. We can define *agapē*-love as 'a commitment to another that motivates us to act on his or her behalf'. Its essence in a church context lies in saying to someone, 'Brother/Sister, I want you to know that I'm committed to you. You'll never knowingly suffer at my hands. I'll never say or do anything, knowingly, to hurt you. I'll always seek to help you and support you . . . No matter what I find out about you, and no matter what happens in the future, either good or bad, my commitment to you will never change . . . I love you, and that's what it means.' [10]

Every church faces a major challenge here as the continuing fact of our fallen natures means that we are often, humanly speaking, both unattractive and unlovable. Hence there is a need in every Christian community for a baptism of *agapē*. The challenge for new-humanity congregations is certainly no less. Our commitment to embrace the widest human diversities means the huge challenge of overcoming our natural human tendency to withdraw from, or at least to hold back from, those who are different from ourselves. The presence of 'strangers' fills us with anxiety, and our ignorance of them and their possible reactions to us paralyses our instinct for love and causes us to back away in fear. But these challenges *can* be overcome, as testimonies like the following one indicate.

> My name is Tatania, and I come from Slovakia. When I arrived in Canada with my mom we did not know any believers. Just before Easter we received an invitation to the Easter service at the Orpheum Theatre. It was wonderful and from then on we began to attend church every Sunday. At the church we found true Christian fellowship. We found open hearts and loving, caring people. They knew how we felt, and I was grateful for the many invitations to their homes. They offered us help and they prayed for us too. We needed to study English and I was introduced to the ESL classes at 'Hobbit House', which are a ministry of the church. I met Marg, who was a leader there. She was so kind, thoughtful and understanding. We became part of the Hobbit House 'family'. I also made friends with a dear lady called Kate. We share our burdens with one another, we rejoice and sorrow together . . . This past couple of years I have experienced so much love and care from the people of the church.

How can we learn to love others, as Christ loved us? Several things are important.

### Love is a gift

If we find ourselves responding to the Bible's description of *agapē*-love with the feeling that it's very difficult, we are getting the message very well. But in fact we would be wrong in so reacting. *Agapē*-love is not just difficult, it is impossible. Only God can consistently love others in the manner that is shown at the cross. Only God can love like God, and so if our love is even remotely to reflect his, he has to help us. But the good news is that he has promised to do so. We are, Paul writes to the Thessalonians, 'taught by God to love each other' (1 Thess. 4:9). More specifically, he sets the Holy Spirit of love within our hearts: 'God has poured out his love [*agapē*] into our hearts by the Holy Spirit' (Rom. 5:5). Love is a 'fruit of the Spirit' (Gal. 5:22), whose ministry in the local church is the crucial context of Paul's magnificent exposition of the contours and colours of love in 1 Corinthians 13, the 'most excellent way' (1 Cor. 12:31). Love is a gift! Hence we ought never to despair totally, even in those moments when our loveless hearts are exposed in their sorry malignity.

Gerd Thiessen, having noted the astonishing optimism of the early believers as far as the achieving of genuine diversity in community is concerned, comments:

> How could the [early Christian] movement cherish the hope of permeating the whole of society with this pattern? Was that not to expect a miracle? And indeed a miracle is what they hoped for. The Jesus movement believed in miracles, in the realization of what appeared to be impossible ... Would not the faith which moves mountains (Mark 11:23) also be capable of changing the human heart? If so many miracles had taken place, would not the miracle of love be possible also?[11]

### Being 'filled' with the Spirit

Every Christian is called to 'be filled with the Spirit' (Eph. 5:18). The essential meaning of the verb here is 'come under the control of'. We are to live in such a way that God's gracious Spirit is our director and guide. It means, as Paul puts it elsewhere, keeping 'in step with the Spirit' (Gal. 5:25). Such a walk will necessarily be a love-walk – which provides a useful barometer of its authenticity, whether in ourselves or in others. We all need regularly to open ourselves consciously to the lordship of the Holy Spirit, and invite him to 'fill' us with his presence and power.

### Seeing them in Christ

Another potent 'love-promoter' is learning to see our fellow Christians in Christ (Rom. 16:2). It will help focus this point in the next few minutes if we hold a picture in our minds of the members of our local church whom we regularly find it most difficult to love. To see them in Christ means consciously to refuse to accept a purely human view of them, but instead to affirm three truths about them.

Firstly, *these are people for whom Christ died*. This is exactly Paul's reminder concerning difficult saints in Romans 14:15 and 1 Corinthians 8:11 (cf. also Rom. 15:7). However unattractive to us, God's estimate of their value is nothing less than that expressed in giving his Son to die in their place at Calvary. In other words, if these people were put 'on sale' in God's universe, we would have to put the cross on their price tag.

Secondly, *these are people in whom Christ now lives.* Paul discovered this truth to his total consternation when he met Jesus outside Damascus: 'Why do you persecute *me?*' (Acts 9:4, my italics). The same truth is reflected in the parable of the sheep and the goats: 'Whatever you did for one of the least of these brothers and sisters of mine, you did for me' (Matt. 25:40, 45). However overlaid the Lord's presence may appear to us, he is nonetheless resident and enthroned in these lives also. To reject these brothers or sisters is, in a real sense, to reject Jesus.

Thirdly, *these are people through whom Christ will one day reign.* All Christians, including the most unattractive believer of our acquaintance, will one day be 'like Christ' (1 John 3:2; 2 Cor. 3:18). In other words, if we could see them now as they will appear then, we would have the greatest difficulty in restraining the impulse to fall at their feet in worship.

### Remember to forget

So many of the barriers between Christians, which bedevil and hamper congregational witness, are harboured memories of past hurts. We are let down in a certain circumstance, even deliberately hurt and rejected – or at least that is how we interpret what happened. And do we let it go, do we forgive and forget? Not for a moment. We hang on to our hurt, even 'nurse it to keep it warm', in Robert Burns' insightful line. Every time we meet with, or even see, that particular sister or brother, it is there, like a mask covering his or her face, behind which his or her real face has ceased to be visible. We can all identify with this.

What can we do about it? Two things can help.

The first is to ponder regularly and long Jesus' parable of the two debtors in Matthew 18:21–35. The man who owed the immense debt is you and I; the one who has forgiven us in the almost absurd kindness of grace is the Lord; the second and, by comparison, 'trivial' debtor is that Christian sister or brother. We read, and ponder, and pray.

Secondly, we consciously and earnestly pray for the one who has wronged us. Instead of talking about him or her to ourselves or to others, we begin regularly to talk about him or her to the Lord. The reference to forgiving and forgetting, above, is no doubt unrealistic, particularly where the hurt has been very deep. As Martin Luther King Jr notes, 'Certainly one can never forget, if that means erasing it totally from the mind. But when we forgive we forget in the sense that the evil deed is no longer a mental block impeding a new relationship.' And he adds (and he surely earned the right to challenge us at this point): 'The degree to which we are able to forgive is the degree to which we are able to love.'[12]

The possibilities of prayer here are well illustrated by Billy Graham.

> I remember an experience in Scotland. Before great crowds of people an American spoke against me. He had said this and that. He had warned the people of Scotland against me. Much of what he said was untrue. I felt it, but never said anything publicly or privately, but it was in my heart. I remember this thing came before me while I was preaching. The Lord said to me, 'You cannot go back to the platform until this is made right.' I wrote that man a letter at 2.00 a.m. after much prayer. God gave me a love for that man which flooded my soul. He still preaches against me. But from that hour God gave me victory. If there is someone you do not understand, get on your knees until God floods your soul with love for him. This is what we need.[13]

## Corporate prayer

'Disciples ... should always pray and not give up' (Luke 18:1). The practice of 'praying together' has very much to contribute to the promotion of a spirit of love, as Pentecost clearly demonstrated. Churches that enjoy a vital and well-supported corporate prayer life are the more likely to experience the special ministry of God's Spirit in their life and witness. It is important that the ministry vision of a congregation includes this element, not only because of its being the promised medium of spiritual blessing in its life and work, but also from the enriched experience of community which arises from spending time together in prayer and engaging together in prayer warfare.

Again, the new-humanity congregation stands to gain much here. It is very helpful if the prayer meetings are also schools of prayer where new Christians can learn how to pray in public and receive the encouragement that comes from that experience. Imagination needs to be used to attain these ends; for instance, topic sheets may be issued; sheets with some of the great prayers of the ages may be printed and given out; the meeting could break into smaller groups where there is less pressure or feeling of self-consciousness; there could be moments of rest and quiet, or of praise and worship, and so on.

The physical setting of prayer gatherings is also important; draughty, uncomfortable and dingy halls should be outlawed, and overly long prayers, if they are discouraging other, humbler particip- ants, may need to be sensitively but firmly handled. Special times of waiting on God, such as nights or half-nights of prayer or prayer retreats, are of great value; though an additional goal should be the development of a 'praying culture' through the church as a whole, so that turning to God together in prayer becomes a natural instinct in all the congregation's life.

Whether we consider the matter personally or corporately, it is difficult to escape the conclusion, as Murray McCheyne put it, that 'what we are on our knees before God, that is what we are, no more and no less'. Prayer is accordingly an irreplaceable promoter of mature discipleship and deepened fellowship, in new-humanity congregations no less than any others.

## Learning to die

Paul exemplifies this inner secret of new-humanity living in his statement that 'death is at work in us, but life is at work in you' (2 Cor. 4:12). As Paul and his fellow apostles experienced the 'daily dying' of the privations listed in the previous verses – pressures, perplexities, persecutions and punches (4:8–9) – so 'life', in the form of salvation, hope, strength and, not least, love, blossomed into existence in the lives of his readers in Corinth (cf. John 12:24–26).

Janet was a special member of her congregation. Again and again she graciously turned aside approaches to serve on one of the church committees or in the leadership of some ministry. The reason she gave was always the same: God had given her a ministry of caring for the especially needy ones, and she had to be free for that. And so, Sunday by Sunday and in all kinds of settings, she could be seen, entirely unselfconsciously, and with no fanfare to attract attention, seated with someone in need. Sometimes you would run into her in a café, or on a park bench, listening, loving, caring, encouraging.

It would be tempting to conclude that that was simply the kind of personality she had naturally; but that would not have told the real story. For Janet was a woman for whom life had not held out its glittering prizes, despite her highly developed professional skills. She had never been allowed the marriage she had longed for; illness sapped her energies and finally took her life prematurely. But behind it all lay her inner secret, a profound love for Jesus Christ and a wholehearted commitment to serve him as she met him in his needy ones. Again and again she had learned, in good times and bad, to give herself to him, no matter how costly. She was someone who had lived out 'the way of the cross'. And so she became a new-humanity person, in whose life people sensed, and were warmed by, the presence of Christ.

### Death and resurrection

The inner, hidden, daily carrying of the cross and the powerful, outward ministry of compassionate care are two sides of the same coin. People like Janet, who love others, not least the unlovely and the marginalized, are made, not born. They are created at the foot of the cross by a thousand daily self-denials for Jesus' sake.

Part of the reason we are not more open to others and to their burdens and crying needs is that, quite simply, we are too preoccupied with ourselves. There are deaths to ourselves – our comforts, our reputation, our self-gratifications, our pride, our store of things, and the hoarding of our time – that we have refused to die.

Anna Laetitia Waring's lines are searching in their challenge:

> I ask thee for a thoughtful love,
> Through constant watching wise,
> To meet the glad with joyful smiles,
> And wipe the weeping eyes;
> And a heart at leisure from itself,
> To soothe and sympathize.[14]

Calvin, in a paragraph of his monumental *Institutes* entitled 'Self-renunciation leads to proper helpfulness towards our neighbour', writes: 'In seeking to benefit one's neighbour, how difficult it is to do one's duty! Unless you give up all thought of self, and, so to speak, get out of yourself, you will accomplish nothing here.'[15]

To 'get out of yourself' – there is the secret! To learn to die to self is to learn to love.

# 9 A heart for the world

*Mission and evangelism in a new-humanity congregation*

'The church *is* mission' was a slogan of the 1970s. It is of course an overstatement, as the last two chapters have in their way underlined. Nonetheless, the Great Commission, which mandates the proclaiming of the gospel to every person everywhere, and the Great Commandments, which refer to sacrificial love of our neighbours whatever their need, are fundamental obligations for any Christian community that claims Jesus as Lord.

So consistent is the New Testament's emphasis on mission as the life blood of the church that no congregational model deserves an audience if it fails to demonstrate its viability as a promoter of mission. That is as true for a new-humanity model as for any other. This is the more important as it is precisely at this point that church models that emphasize community as a primary value (such as the new-humanity) have come in for criticism. Fully to sustain our case, we need to offer some response to these concerns before more positively demonstrating the great missional potential of the new-humanity way.

***Does the stress on community not lead to self-preoccupation; to being a church 'for itself' rather than for God and the world?***

Human nature being what it is, this criticism focuses a genuine danger. However, there appears to be no necessary reason to create this antithesis as far as new-humanity congregations are concerned; quite the contrary, as we shall argue later.

The explicit commitment to diversity, the fundamental feature of new-humanity congregations, roots an outward-looking instinct right at the core of such churches. To operate with a congregational culture of inclusiveness of the other who is different from ourselves, and who exists beyond our normal boundaries of connection, means there is no possibility of a navel-gazing preoccupation becoming entrenched. In fact, because of this watermark feature, new-humanity congregations are arguably the least likely to become self-preoccupied.

Indeed, the sensitivity to the 'different other' which the new-humanity congregation embodies becomes a natural point of connection with the needs of the neighbourhood, as well as with the tragic victims who lie in their multitudes on the doorsteps of the nations. New-humanity congregations learn to listen to those whose skin is a different colour, whose language and customs are different, and who have different opportunities and priorities, and different needs clamouring to be addressed. New-humanity congregations, if they are true to their birthright, exist in a culture of caring which makes the accusation of self-preoccupation impossible to sustain.

*Does this 'diversity-in-unity' communal model not founder on the fact that most people do not want to be exposed to people different from themselves?*

We respond *firstly* with a procedural issue. Where do we look for direction in building congregations? Are the results of sociological research what should determine our methods? Do we simply look at what seems to work in practice, to what appears to make churches grow bigger? Or do we retain our historic evangelical orientation, and, as with any other issue in Christian faith and practice, consult what God says on the matter in Scripture? As Edmund Clowney notes, 'If our growing understanding of sociology outstrips our grasp of biblical theology, we may seek to build Christ's church from the wrong blueprints.'

*The Bible says . . .*

**Secondly,** we have been at pains to demonstrate, in the first section of this book, that God's blueprint in Scripture calls for congregations that are centres of reconciliation, counter-cultural communities, producing a quality of life that is finally explicable only in terms of God's supernatural presence.

> For the church to embody into its structures the separations of race, class, language, or sex is to deny the gospel which reconciles. The church is not a unity of one culture, but a unity amid diversity (1 Cor. 12:4–11), one body with many members (1 Cor. 12:12–13), reconciled individuals who live in peace (Eph. 2:11–22). The fullest expression of that reality is the church of multi-cultural persons who worship, serve, and fellowship with each other in the unity of their faith in Christ without the sacrifice of their personal identities.[1]

**Thirdly,** the attempt to plane down to a minimum the cost of becoming disciples of Jesus in order to make the commitment more attractive runs into serious difficulty with the terms set by Jesus. 'If anyone comes to me and does not hate father and mother, wife and children, brothers and sisters – yes, even life itself – such a person cannot be my disciple . . . those of you who do not give up everything you have cannot be my disciples' (Luke 14:26, 33; cf. Matt. 16:24–26).

Nor did Jesus leave this at the theoretical level, as 'a certain ruler' found out to his cost: 'Sell everything you have and give to the poor, and you will have treasure in heaven. Then come, follow me' (Luke 18:18, 22; cf. 9:57–62). The text underlines Jesus' love for the man (Mark 10:21), and hence, no doubt, his sorrow when the ruler was unprepared for the sacrifice demanded. But Jesus let him go. Jesus would not countenance a discipleship that is not ready to give up a self-centred, self-pleasing lifestyle. Quite simply, making it as easy as possible is nowhere on Jesus' radar screen.

Lest this be thought unrealistically severe, we simply draw attention to the fact that all who subsequently were numbered with Jesus and the Christian community passed through the rite of baptism in accordance with the command of Jesus (Matt. 28:19–20; Acts 2:38, 41; etc.). Baptism, as Paul makes clear, involves a radical self-denial, a dying and being crucified with Christ (Rom. 6:1–11; Gal. 2:20; Col. 2:12). Thus, concerns that potential disciples' personal comfort zone should not be violated appear to be in conflict with the terms of commitment laid down by Jesus and adhered to in the New Testament church.

American preacher Will Campbell tells the story of his baptism in the East Forks River in Amite County, Mississippi. Will's brother Joe was a bit of a sceptic. Joe stood on the bank, watching the preacher baptizing two or three other people before Will's turn. As he watched, he grew more and more worried for Will's safety. So he slid down the muddy bank and grabbed Will, saying, 'Will, dear God, don't let them do this to you. A fellow could get killed doing this.'

Will said, 'It took me thirty years to recognize that was precisely the point.'[2]

### The blood of the martyrs

This point is borne out by the history of the church over the centuries. When, in times of violent persecution, commitment to Christ has literally called for death, the church has commonly grown and expanded. One need look no further than the miracle of the church in China today, bearing in mind the history of that nation over the last fifty years. Correspondingly, when the cost has been minimized to accommodate personal tastes and traditional securities, the church has commonly languished in decline. One need only think of the history of the church on the western side of Europe's Iron Curtain over the same fifty-year time-span.

### Repent and believe

**Fourthly**, putting this still another way, the sociologically determined formula of minimum social discomfort for entry to the church implies that there are certain areas of the individual's personal life and relationships that are exempted from the call to repentance, which is the prelude to commitment (Luke 3:3–14; 13:1–5; Mark 1:15; Acts 2:38; 20:21). Thus, potential converts need to repent of dishonesty, greed and immorality, but, it would seem, not of racial or cultural pride, or pride of generation or social status. But a repentance that is partial is no repentance at all. The image of death is to the point; death, by definition, covers every aspect of a person's consciousness and all his or her relationships and loyalties. And the price of entry to Christ's community, for Jesus and the apostles, is exactly that – death.

The New Testament knows nothing of a Gospel that makes a divorce between ... communion with God and communion with one's neighbour, between faith and works. The Cross is not only the negation of every human effort to gain God's favour by works of the law; it is also the demand for a new quality of life characterized by love – the opposite of an individualistic life, centred on personal ambitions, indifferent to the needs of others.[3]

The issue here becomes quite simple. Jesus puts it in a question: 'Why do you call me, "Lord, Lord," and do not do what I say?' (Luke 6:46). It is not our place to adjust the terms of entry to God's community to the point where our contemporaries feel personally comfortable. If Scripture informs us that the community of Christ is, by the will and good purpose of God, to be a diverse body, and that by that very fact it will honour and glorify the Lord and magnify the cross-work of his dear Son, then we dare not set aside that characteristic.

**What do we do with the claimed evidence from sociology that, since diverse groups are often less cohesive, they are weaker and less able to generate growth?**

'As churches constitute themselves agents to produce social change they are likely to lose, rather than gain, social strength.'[4] This claim is one of the justifications offered in the United States for the development of racially divided congregations, explored in the recent work of Michael O. Emerson and Christian Smith, *Divided by Faith*.[5] This study has demonstrated, with considerable plausibility, that the willingness of evangelical Christians in the United States to accept a separate congregational policy with respect to the critical racial divide between blacks and whites, and whites and people of colour generally, has resulted in the entrenchment of that biblically embarrassing divide. The fact that 90% of American congregations are made up of at least 90% of the same race is disturbing in a nation that claims a massive proportion of professedly born-again Christians.

*The purpose of it all*
This regrettable development raises a fundamental question: What is the ultimate purpose of the church? Why do we form churches at all,

and encourage their growth? The only finally defensible answer is: Because we seek the honour and glory of God.

Building statistically growing churches is no doubt a critical means to that greatest of ends; but it is only one – the Bible does not consist only of the Great Commission. It consists of sixty-six books, all divinely inspired and God-breathed. God speaks in all of these books to all his people all of the time. Hence we need to ask of the whole Bible: How do we honour, love and glorify God? The answer is clear: By reflecting him in our lives, personally and collectively. Sharing the good news of who he is and what he has done for the world in the Lord Jesus Christ is a major part of that, but honouring God also involves acts of worship, living godly (= Godlike) lives, obeying all his commands, ministering with compassion in his name to all the needy of the world, living in all things for his praise, and fulfilling and becoming all he has given us to be.

In other words, the goal of the church is also about the quality of our lives as well as quantity of our conversions. When the qualitative criterion is applied, segregated congregations cease to be validated, and especially so when they are developed in the midst of a society where racial segregation, and the social and economic injustices to which it gives rise, are, to any unbiased observer, a highly evident feature of that society.

### Counter-culture community

It is clear from the New Testament that what authenticated the witness of the early Christian evangelists was not a conscious effort to limit the degree to which their church life was counter-cultural, but rather, in step with Jesus' prescription for effective mission, the ministry of the Holy Spirit: 'When he comes, he will convict the world of guilt in regard to sin and righteousness and judgment' (John 16:8). How did the Spirit do this? By coming upon the community of faith, normatively demonstrated in his coming at Pentecost. This 'coming upon them' produced overwhelming guilt in the hearers – no surprise there: 'When the people heard this, they were cut to the heart and said to Peter and the other apostles, "Brothers, what shall we do?" ' (Acts 2:37). But that Holy Spirit visitation was certainly not an endorsement of a policy of conformity to the community; quite the reverse, as the references to waiting in prayer (1:14) and supernatural manifestations, including tongues-speaking (2:1–12), make clear.

We all stand in daily need of that divine authentication of our evangelistic witness, I as much as any other preacher and witness. The means remain exactly the same: the coming of the Holy Spirit upon the community of faith in answer to believing prayer.

Further, while there may be sociological support for the idea that, among some groups in certain places, a stress on diversity might hinder the fostering of a strong group identity and result in a reduced ability to grow, we must also weigh the accumulated experience of the early Christian centuries that we have documented earlier. These first generations of Christians, ignorant of the finer points of sociology, but fired by the *agapē*-love of the Holy Spirit, crossed all the boundaries and drew people in astonishing numbers to Christ by their very ability to embrace diversity. The reference here to the Holy Spirit is surely critical. We are not talking about social groups in general, but about a supernatural agency, the divine community created and indwelt by the living God.

Besides, the sociological evidence is less than universal. In our setting here in Vancouver, for example, on the same continent and in the same time period, the emergence in our congregation of bewildering social diversity actually deepened mutual commitment, and was a major engine driving significant growth.

*A diversity tsunami*
But another factor has recently entered the picture, one which demands a revision of these negative instincts about diversity-embracing congregations: the accumulating evidence of accelerating social diversity in all our global cultures.[6]

The world in which these justifications of segregated congregations were framed is in fact fast disappearing; the world of tomorrow will be very different, but wonderfully, in the process, it will afford new opportunities to obey God's Word and discover in the process the God-honouring joy and richness of multi-racial, multi-everything church life. All the projections of tomorrow's global societies indicate the inevitability of social diversity as never before. There will simply be fewer and fewer ghettos of 'my kind of people' to hide in, and churches organized around that principle will, with time, face the danger of becoming symbols of nostalgic antiquity.

*'United by faith'*
The issues raised for the American church by *Divided by Faith* have been responded to recently in *United by Faith: The Multicultural Congregation as an Answer to the Problem of Race*. Its authors recognize the force of the biblical case for heterogeneity made in our earlier chapters, as well as the soundness of the argument presented in *Divided by Faith* concerning the critical nature of the racial problem. Their starting point for a solution is for congregations to become *intentionally multi-racial*. In essence, 'all American churches should be multiracial'.[7]

'The future of Christianity in the 21st century depends on practical living examples of authentic reconciling faith. While multiracial congregations will never be perfect organizations, God's call to reconciliation through the life, death and resurrection and abiding presence of Jesus Christ compels us to embrace the challenge of moving forward toward this goal.'[8] This represents a significant agreement with the case argued in this book.

Having responded to these questions, it is time to complete the picture by expounding the positive potential for mission of new-humanity, diversity-in-unity, together-under-Christ congregations.

## New-humanity missional potential

### Coming home
In practice, new-humanity congregations *are* wonderfully attractive. In serving in such a setting during my years of ministry in Vancouver, I lost count of the number of times a new congregant said to me, 'Whenever I came in here I felt I had come home'. In most of these cases the speakers had no previous history of Christian involvement. They were neither anti-religious nor committed in any significant degree to a religious world view. They were, in many cases, representatives of the neo-paganism of postmodern Western society. But they felt at home. Clearly, something was going on at a deep level of their consciousness, some elemental sense of a place called 'home', where the human family could accept and embrace one another beyond the superficial diversities that polarize and separate. In finding

themselves in a community where these differences had ceased to be important, their hearts resonated to it, and they found awakened within them a longing and a sense of belonging, a sense of being at home. Their name is legion in these dawning years of the twenty-first century.

### 'Otherism'

How do we reach out to the range of people who surround our churches? At the root of effective outreach is a specific attitude; we referred to it in the previous chapter as the secret of effective fellowship; and it is no different for effective mission: the attitude is *love*. 'I can't hear what you say until I see that you care' is a fair summary of where many in our communities are coming from today.

Let's not be under any illusion here; such loving is costly. John warns us of that: 'Love must not be a matter of words or talk; it must be genuine, and show itself in action' (1 John 3:18, New English Bible). But making space in our lives really to care about others and to allow their agendas to invade and even supersede our own is critical if we are serious about seeing them join us among the followers of Jesus.

Luci Shaw, the American poet quoted earlier, in her book *God in the Dark*, tells the moving story of the death from throat cancer of her husband, Harold. During the final weeks of his life they often took a walk together in their neighbourhood.

> On one of our evening strolls down St Charles Road we saw Lindy, our young neighbour. We stopped and talked to her. Today a letter came:
>
> > 'I'm not sure what's leading me to write but tonight, when I talked with you both, something inside me reached out to you. I saw you walking, arm in arm, and it brought tears to my eyes ... For twenty-two years I've despised everything to do with Christianity and God. Last year the hypocrisy of it all came out and more than ever I doubted. I wanted to end my life last summer because of what happened between my parents, but I refused to give up. A couple of months ago I decided that I would quit trying to find happiness aside from God, and told myself I'd give up everything if only I could be sure that he is real ... Tonight I saw and felt God in your presence.

When you told me, Mr. Shaw, that you were praying for us, I
almost fainted. You, coming so close to dying. You, praying for us.
I just wanted you to know that seeing you both walking down the
hill and loving each other fills my heart like nothing else. You are
proof that God does not walk away from marriage, and you didn't
walk away from God ... Though I am now only a beginner at this,
I do believe that God wanted me to take out the garbage tonight.

'Love, Lindy'[9]

Here is the essence of that selfless attitude that wins others to
Christ, as Lindy was drawn to him here. In a place where self-
preoccupation was only to be expected, there was 'a heart at leisure
from itself, to sooth and sympathize', with eternal results.

*Love irresistible*
The new-humanity congregation is committed to caring, and that in
turn produces an atmosphere of care. We encounter here a practical
application of Jesus' words in John 17 – what might not unfairly be
entitled 'Jesus' prescription for evangelistic effectiveness' – 'that all
of them may be one ... so that the world may believe that you have
sent me' (verse 21; cf. verse 23). The persuasiveness of the preaching
of the gospel of reconciliation with God is conditioned by the degree of
the experience of reconciliation in the congregation in whose presence,
and on whose behalf, the message is being proclaimed.

*The final apologetic*
A congregation where something of the love of the Spirit is expressed
will be a place where the gospel can grow wings and take flight
into the minds and hearts of those who have yet to respond to its
summons. New-humanity congregations are dedicated to the expression of such love, and so are accordingly places where the gospel will
have power. I used to say in Vancouver that 'the best evangelist in
this church is this church'; and it was true, and can be true for every
church.

No-one, or very few, can for ever resist the appeal of love. We were
made by it, and we were made for it. Reynolds Price speaks of 'the
sentence that mankind craves from stories – *the Maker of all things loves*

*and wants me*.[10] He is referring to the elemental human longing for love. Mother Teresa articulates it movingly:

> People today are hungry for love, for understanding love which is the only answer to loneliness and great poverty ... people are suffering from terrible despair, terrible hatred ... They have forgotten how to smile, they have forgotten the beauty of the human touch. They are forgetting what is human love. They need someone who will love and respect them.[11]

Churches who have discovered the love of God poured out into their hearts (Rom. 5:5) will, sooner or later, experience without fail the reality of evangelistic potency. To return again to Jess Moody's words: 'People do not go where the action is; they go where the love is.'

> Urban people want, and hunger for, fellowship which is high quality and lasting. Neighbourhood taverns function as the therapy and fellowship centers night after night for many people. If you study these, you will find that drinking is incidental to the real purpose of the gathering. When Ralph Neighbour studied taverns in Houston, Texas, he concluded that people came looking for fellowship and a shoulder to cry on. Urban people protect themselves with casual, superficial relationships, because urban life is socially mobile ... [but] at the same time, they need a few continuing relationships in all kinds of settings.[12]

They need to be loved!

### Multi-layered outreach

Another dimension of new-humanity missional effectiveness lies in the diversity of its constituents. Their breadth of type becomes the basis for an outreach that is similarly multi-layered. In a culture of massive diversity, the best possible agent for mission is surely a congregation with a corresponding breadth.

Such a climate calls for the conveying of a clear message that the church does not exist for only one type of person or, what is worse, 'our' type of person.

If the members of the congregation all wear suits, and then the pastor in the pulpit asks people to come to Christ, there is a real danger that the sub-text is – 'You can come to Christ, but you must all dress like us.' I saw churches in India with full parking lots and walls around them. The pastor is preaching, 'Come to Jesus,' but the behavior system of the church is saying, 'We are not of this community. You can come to Christ if you are of our social class.'[13]

The diversity of the new-humanity congregation gives an unmistakable message: this gospel and this Saviour really are for *everybody*.

Long gone are the days when evangelism could be reduced to a single method or means, whether the preaching from the pulpit or the outreach of a well-developed Sunday school or a vibrant youth group. Each of these will continue to be a means of grace to some as they grope their way towards a living faith. But they will be joined by ministries as diverse as free meals for street folk, classes teaching English as a second language, Christian theatre productions, a Christianity Explored or Alpha course, seven-step groups for the overweight, home-movie evenings, Agnostics Anonymous discussion groups, cycling weekends, street ministry for homeless young people, classes on good financial management, occasions celebrating the contribution of a local hospital emergency department or of local schoolteachers, firemen, police officers or social workers.

The list is endless; the doors into the kingdom are as multiple. Our experience in such a congregational context was that the more doors into the kingdom we opened, the more people came through them. But only a diverse congregation can operate such a multi-faceted mission.

### Holistic people for holistic mission

A further advantage of the consciously inclusive, new-humanity congregation in the area of mission is its natural instinct to respond to the full range of human need. Holistic mission, in which the Great Commission to proclaim the gospel is complemented by the Great Commandment to love our neighbour, is the natural outflow.

There is a sense of authenticity in preaching the saving love of God in the context of a group of people in wheelchairs whose presence signals the warm inclusion of people of all kinds of disability and need, and when in the same context the message is translated into sign language for a group of deaf people. I am reminded here of a Scottish friend who, when a profoundly deaf enquirer began to attend his church, learned sign language in order to befriend and share Christ with him. Once that spirit of caring takes root, the possibilities are endless.

Following a suggestion of Ray Bakke, our congregation in Vancouver stumbled upon a remarkably fruitful outreach medium, based on just such holistic concern. It is a medium that has potential for many other congregations. It all boils down to saying, 'Thank you.'

For a year or two the church had filled a historic downtown theatre for its Easter Sunday celebration, drawing between two and three thousand each year. We featured it annually as a Community Service, widely publicized as open to, and designed for, the whole urban core community. Ray's idea was to select a group that offered a significant service to the community all year round, and to thank them publicly during the celebration. And so we launched the First Baptist Annual Community Service Award. We began with the emergency department of our local hospital and moved on to the staff of our local schools, our police department, our firemen, our downtown social workers, the team serving meals to street people year-round, and so on.

In each case we informed the agency in advance of their having been selected as the recipients of the award for that year, and invited them to send appropriate representatives to receive the award plaque during the service. Invariably, the top leadership of the organization came to do the honours, always accompanied by significant numbers of their 'other ranks' with their families. The neutral setting, the thrilling Easter music and choral singing by all ages, the simple, clear testimonies to a living Christ, and the forthright sharing of the Easter message in preaching all came together in a remarkably effective way of sharing the good news, and of genuinely expressing our debt to frequently unappreciated public servants.

I will never forget the year the city police Downtown Unit was honoured. They had been taking some criticism in the press at the time. When, after an appropriate citation, the award plaque was presented to two senior city police officers, the packed audience rose spontaneously and gave their chiefs of police a prolonged standing ovation. I had never before observed two tough, six-foot-plus police veterans in tears!

It soon became apparent that year by year we were thanking people who were almost never appreciated publicly for their service, and hence were actually discharging a genuine public debt. And into the bargain we were able to share the Easter message in a way that, over the years, drew numbers to a living faith in the Easter Saviour.

## World mission

The diversity of a new-humanity congregation also links it in a very natural way to the church's global mission. It is not difficult to stir interest in Christian witness in say, Eastern Europe, or in the northern provinces of China, when members of the congregation have their personal roots in these places, and have family and other connections there; or to generate concern for those suffering human-rights abuses in North Korea when the congregation has a number of Koreans within its membership.

## A larger Christ

I recall a conversation with a mayor of Vancouver. I asked him if he could tell me of one other group, meeting anywhere in our city on a weekly basis, for whatever purpose, with a greater diversity than that reflected in the congregation of First Baptist.

He thought for a while; he was a very good mayor who knew his city well. Finally, he replied, 'No, I don't think I can.'

Whereupon I was able to say to him, gently and sincerely: 'Doesn't that say something very important about Jesus Christ?'

In John 12:32, Jesus, in the shadow of Calvary, makes this claim: 'I, when I am lifted up from the earth, will draw all people to myself.' The Lord, 'lifted up' in holy sacrifice, draws the nations to himself.

A final reason for celebrating congregational diversity in the sphere of mission is the implications that it generates for our vision of Jesus himself. Peruvian missiologist Samuel Escobar captures it memorably.

> The missionary facts of our time make me pause in wonder. Jesus Christ, incarnate Son of God, is the core of the gospel, which as a potent seed has flourished in a thousand different plants. We can name a place and a time on earth in which Jesus lived and taught. In other words we can place him in a particular culture at a particular moment in history. 'The Word became flesh and lived for a while among us,'

in Palestine during the first century of our era. After that, the story of Jesus has moved from culture to culture, from nation to nation, from people to people. And something very wonderful has taken place. Though this Jesus was a peasant from Palestine, everywhere he has been received, loved, and adored, and people in hundreds of cultures and languages have come to see the glory of God in the face of Jesus Christ. Moreover they have come to feel that Jesus is 'theirs,' so that they say, 'Jesus is one of ours.'[14]

That wonder, the universal attractiveness of Jesus, can be powerfully experienced in a missional context in which, by God's marvellous grace, he can be seen, still at work, drawing the nations in all their diversity to himself. Take away the diversity of the missional community, and you rob yourself of this wonderful dimension, not only of authentication of the truth of the gospel, as we noted above, but also of extending the honour and praise of the one who is the Lord of all the nations. The result is simply, yet wonderfully – a larger, greater, more adorable Jesus Christ.

### All kinds of diversity

In the discussion of the alleged missional liabilities and the actual missional advantages of new-humanity congregations, stress has necessarily fallen on the racial and ethnic mix. That parameter of diversity formed the paradigm model for our biblical argument as we examined Ephesians 2:11–18, and it is probably the feature of inclusiveness that most obviously strikes a visitor to a new-humanity congregation.

However, it is important to underline again that the case we are making here is not confined to the racial or ethnic dimension. As we saw from the biblical evidence, God's plan is for all diversities to be brought together under the lordship of Christ: 'all things . . . together under one head, even Christ' (Eph. 1:10). That is where the honour of God arises and the supernatural ministry of the Holy Spirit is truly manifested.

It does not take a moment's reflection to accept the force of this. How could the God who made us such multi-dimensional persons rest content with uniting us only in terms of race and ethnicity? So, *all* primary diversities need to be part of our vision, and part accordingly of the healing and transforming work of the Holy Spirit in the church, moving us towards the glorious end of being together: a bride 'without stain or wrinkle or any other blemish', 'beautifully dressed for her husband' (Eph. 5:27; Rev. 21:2).

This has an immediate practical relevance, for, in some locations, particularly rural ones, only one racial group resides. In such cases a multi-racial, multi-ethnic congregation is hardly a possibility. However, this does not mean that a biblical new-humanity church is impossible. There are all the other dimensions of diversity to be embraced as fully in such settings as in any others. Hence the diversities of age, social status, family unit, wealth, religious history, personality, and mental and physical health all wait to be addressed, and the overcoming of them offers no less a richness of communal, God-honouring congregational experience as a result.

Thus, in conclusion, in the area of the church's mission no less than in the areas of worship, leadership, discipleship and fellowship, the new-humanity congregation vindicates itself as offering authentic New Testament forms of Christian experience and practice. New-humanity congregations are evangelistic congregations.

The diversity-in-community congregation a hindrance to effective mission? Don't you believe it! The exact reverse is true.

## 10  Riding the wave

*The challenges and opportunities of new-humanity churches
in today's and tomorrow's worlds*

'Do not merely listen to the Word ... Do what it says,' writes James
(James 1:22). In the preceding chapters we have presented a case for
the creation of Christian congregations around the world that
consciously embrace diversity. We have argued that such congregations were typical of first-century churches, and that the principles
underlying them are clearly urged upon us in the New Testament. If
we are committed to the great Reformed, evangelical principle of *sola
Scriptura* – that God speaking in the words of Scripture is our supreme
and sufficient authority for the direction of our Christian faith, both
personal and corporate – then new-humanity churches become a
divine mandate.

Diversity is not optional. God's goal for his church, within his all-
embracing purpose 'to bring all things in heaven and on earth together
under one head, even Christ' (Eph. 1:10), calls for congregations where
that final unification is anticipated. If we are concerned, as we surely
should be, to march in step with God's plan for the ages, we will be
in the business of establishing new-humanity churches. The fact that
this is clearly presented to us in Scripture, both in direct didactic
sections and in the constituency of its established churches, and that it

is given further validation in so many primary Christian doctrines, leaves us little choice but to re-examine our present practice in its light.

But even these supreme constraints do not exhaust the case, for, as we saw, this vision of the church as a nucleus of reconciled humanity in the Holy Spirit is profoundly relevant to the opportunities as well as the clamant demands of our global context at the beginning of the third millennium. And that cultural and contextual support is itself given a sharper point by the recognition that in certain key respects the world we 'do church' in today is remarkably paralleled by the first-century setting in which the Christian church burst into existence and carried its mission forward with such effectiveness that, by the late 50s, Paul is informing the Romans that there is no longer any scope for his evangelistic labours in the eastern Empire and he must now seek new, unevangelized territory in the region of Spain (Rom. 15:15–24).[1]

We have noted that the implications of this vision also reach inwards to the achieving of a reconciled, personal identity in Christ, and outwards to the achieving of enhanced relationships between churches. However, the starting point, and certainly the place where the New Testament puts its emphasis, is the local church, and it is there that we, too, need to begin in our response to the new-humanity challenge.

## Not really an option

The global reality of a diversified, multi-cultural, multi-everything world is simply not going to go away. It is our destined future. It is already having an impact on life at every level, and will do so even more profoundly in the next few decades. Howard Snyder, among others, predicts a 'new global society by 2030'.[2] Even as I write these words, along with everyone else on this planet, I am in process; moving from the old three worlds of the twentieth century (First World, Second World, Third World) to the one world – just planet Earth – of the twenty-first.

Indeed, that future is already here. 'The question is not whether there will be a multi-cultural church. Rather the question is whether those who have become accustomed to seeing the gospel expressed only, or primarily, in terms of the dominant cultures of the North Atlantic will be able to participate in the life of the multi-cultural church that is already a reality.'[3]

However my readers may have reacted to the argument presented in these pages, the issue underlying this book is a critical one for every congregation, everywhere. Sometime, somewhere, we shall all need to come to terms with it, hopefully sooner rather than later.

The great good news, however, is that we are not finally at the mercy of sociological or global-political forces. We are in the hands of the Lord God Almighty, who holds the world and reigns over it through his exalted Son, Jesus Christ, the Lord of all. All that we experience today and tomorrow is under his rule, and part of his unfolding purpose for the ages. The future vision we are travelling to meet is finally nothing other than a new vision of the face of God. The 'new world order' is in fact a place of enormous potential for new discoveries of the surpassing power of the universal gospel, and of the riches of his grace mediated through his indestructible, endlessly diverse human family. To open ourselves to it is to walk towards blessing; it is to journey towards the further fulfilments of his glorious purpose of bringing all things together under Christ.

How the principles of the new-humanity church are worked out in each local setting will patently be a matter of very considerable diversity. Every congregation is as unique as the uniqueness of the individual believers who together comprise it. Many factors will affect the outcome, so that new-humanity congregations themselves may look quite different from one another.

## The good and the better

For those who are travelling at this point along a road of principled homogeneity, the challenge is clear: to think again, or, if that seems inappropriately negative, to thank God for the blessings of the past, but to open ourselves to something different, and better, in the future.

That God can work in *all* settings is patent from the briefest glance at Christian history. How could we think otherwise of one with whom 'all things are possible'? How could we think otherwise of a God whose passion to reach and embrace his prodigal creatures is for ever etched in the blood of the cross?

That God *can* work in contexts that contradict his disclosed plan for his church and his world does not, however, justify continuing to pursue a pattern that lacks biblical justification when another biblical and fruitful possibility is available.

Jesus' image in John 15 is to the point. There is a state of 'bearing fruit' which is, of course, pleasing to the Father Gardener's heart (verse 2). But his heart yearns for 'much fruit' (verse 8); so much so that he is apparently prepared to take steps, even painful ones for the branches concerned (verse 2), in order to increase the fruitfulness. In other words, without denying the fruitfulness of homogeneous congregations where God's Word is proclaimed, non-Christians are sought and brought to Christ, godly lives are lived, prayer is offered, and faithful service is rendered – but rather delighting in that fruitfulness – we may surely invite those in such settings to consider the possibility of bearing 'much fruit', an increased faithfulness to God's Word leading to that greater glory for the Father Gardener for which he yearns: 'This is to my Father's glory, that you bear *much* fruit' (verse 8, my italics).

Jesus' further observation is also relevant: those who do so will thus be showing themselves to be his disciples (verse 8). For, as we have attempted to demonstrate, that is what the new-humanity way offers. It is a way of embracing Jesus' full terms for discipleship – to deny self and to take up the cross in following him. It is a way of living out our discipleship by obeying *all* that he has commanded (Matt. 28:20).

In other words, there is a 'good' and a 'better' way to build churches. Like Paul, we need to consider – as well as 'the present way' or the 'good way', or even the 'fruitful way' – 'the most excellent way' (1 Cor. 12:31). We need Paul's spirit in our lives, and not least in our congregational planning and dreaming: 'Not that I have already obtained . . . or have already been made perfect, but I press on to take hold of that for which Christ Jesus took hold of me . . . Forgetting what is behind and straining towards what is ahead, I press on towards the goal to win the prize for which God has called me heavenwards in Christ Jesus' (Phil. 3:12–14).

The challenge of these words is, of course, as real for practitioners of new-humanity churches as for any other followers of Jesus. We are all only 'on the way', and will continually be so throughout our earthly journey. But in the process of that journey to an interface with God's glory in the presence of our returning Lord, there is a way of doing church that carries a clear God-authorized mandate, and which is therefore most likely to maximize the glory we will present to him on that greatest of days.

It is, moreover, a way of doing church that will allow us to be ourselves, not only a localized 'Mexican wave' every passing week in worship, but also, and even more importantly, a place where many of the major human diversities are graciously transcended in a Spirit-generated unity of life; a community of the risen Jesus, together under Christ, and thereby a profoundly relevant witness to the eternal purpose of the ever-blessed God, who, on that coming day, will unite all things 'in heaven and on earth together under one head, even Christ'.


## A new paradigm?

In essence, what we are arguing for here is, for many congregations, a change in what some recent discussion has referred to as the 'myth' or 'metanarrative' of the congregation.[4] Others speak not dissimilarly of a 'paradigm'. The call represented in these chapters is the call, in many cases, for a congregational 'paradigm shift'.[5]

If this seems rather theoretical, even threatening, we can see it simply as the invitation to a congregation to adjust their vision to bring it more clearly into line with the New Testament, by seeing themselves henceforth as a community that will embrace diversity as a worthy, fundamental goal, 'not as a threat to be feared, but as a gift to be celebrated'.[6]

Finally considered, the call to new humanity is a call to the defiance of faith – in the face of the brokenness of existence and the weaknesses and disfigurements of the church, in the face of the burgeoning diversity of the world with its huge potential for conflict, in the face of the unbelief and wanderings of our own hearts and the impending fact of death for all of us – a call to believe, in spite of all that, that God is, that Jesus reigns, and that a radically new, *divine* world order is on its way, in which the people of the triune God will be transformed into a single, new, glorified and everlasting family – and a call to dare to live now in the light of that future. It is a call to be 'an embodied question mark', a group of people who, by the supernatural grace of God, 'live another set of relationships within the given social system',[7] to the glory of our ever-blessed God.

## It's a way forward for today and tomorrow

The last few years have witnessed a rash of publications and discussions, on both sides of the Atlantic, on the future of the church. By their very profusion they bear witness to the widespread sense in many hearts that the church has somehow lost its way in the old Atlantic axis. True, there is considerable activity in many places, Christian institutions operate energetically, and people are coming to faith in Christ out of all the generations. Widely publicized and marketed models of church are out there, and new communities of faith are being formed in numerous places. But the nagging question remains as to what all this amounts to.

The disturbing reality is that, for all this activity and number-crunching, the impact that people who profess the evangelical faith are making on the wider cultures on both sides of the Atlantic is disappointingly small. Even more seriously, as has been painfully documented recently for North American Christianity, the personal lifestyles of those populating evangelical communities are at many points completely indistinguishable from those of their non-Christian fellow citizens.[8]

To visit our typical evangelical churches in these early years of the third millennium is hardly a consistently inspiring experience. The 'worship' is often thin and human-centred, with very little sense of encountering an awesome and transcendent deity in whose hand is our every breath, in whose unpayable debt we live in every moment, and to whom we are finally and personally accountable. The music at times dominates all else, and is too often in the medium of only one or two generations. The critical communications link between the platform and the congregation in the pews is frequently so filtered through technological media as to significantly reduce the spontaneous, natural humanity of the relationship. The preaching is commonly aimed at self-help issues, and there is little unveiling of the greatness and glory of the triune God, little attempt to let loose the massive, liberating, mind-blowing truths of the Scriptures, and little accordingly to inspire the 'inexpressible and glorious joy' (1 Pet. 1:8), which was apparently the regular diet of the first Christian generation. And the quality of our mutual relationships is often so superficial that most congregants would not recognize their fellow worshippers in the adjoining pew if they met them the following morning in a coffee queue.

Is it not time to ask some deep questions, such as: What is the church for? Whose agenda are we attempting to fulfil? What does 'success' mean for churches today, or in any day? Where is God in it all?

The new-humanity model offers a way of doing church that is profoundly rooted in the Scriptures, and so has divine authorization. It is massively relevant to our times, as we have shown. It is profoundly missional and growth-orientated. It holds out the promise of greatly enriched and deepened relationships, as all worshippers of whatever background, gender or generation are affirmed and embraced, to say nothing of the countless delightful relational serendipities of the Holy Spirit which it also promises.

Not least, it is a model that is profoundly doxological, as it spells out a path to service for God's glory, and to worship experiences that can be alive with his presence and Spirit. The new-humanity, diversity-in-unity, together-under-Christ model represents a way forward for the evangelical faith in this time; and it is moreover wonderfully accessible, since any local church anywhere can capture the vision and begin to implement it as God leads them forward. It is a biblical way of doing church whose hour has surely dawned.

### 'I have a dream . . . '

Let the conclusion be a dream.[9]

I have a dream – a dream of a congregation where people of all colours and from every ethnic identity find welcome, warmth, dignity and a sense of belonging; I have a dream of a church where men and women worship the triune God, and serve together as equally valuable in the sight of God, and equal in their capacity to honour him.

I have a dream of a Christian community where children, youth, middle-aged and seniors, boomers, busters, generation-Xers and millennials learn to respect and love and discover their profound need for each other; where people from all wealth and power indexes can live and relate and laugh together.

I have a dream of a family where singles and marrieds, and marrieds with families, and single parents and divorcees are all affirmed in their worth before God and his people; a family where poor and rich, sophisticated and unsophisticated, the physically and mentally strong and the physically and mentally challenged have learned to walk together in love, and to appreciate and affirm each other.

I have a dream of a people of God where differences of personality and huge diversities of spiritual stories and spiritual journeys, or the lack of them, are no barrier to acceptance.

I have a dream of all of that many-splendoured, multi-textured humanity uniting under the conscious, blessed rule of the exalted Lord Jesus Christ through his living, liberating, energizing Word, joining in wondering communion in their worship, along with saints and angels – I have a dream.

And I have a dream of that same exuberant, multi-colour family, swept along by the Holy Spirit, streaming forth from their worship place into the community around them – to throw their arms around it, and hug it to their hearts; offering to all who have need the practical ministries of love – to the poor and the homeless, single parents and street kids, HIV/Aids sufferers and the addicted; and sharing too the joyous good news of Jesus and his great salvation – with the lost and lonely, the affluent and the power-brokers, the cynics and the seekers, the young and the aged, the followers of other faith traditions and the followers of none, local residents and those from every corner of the globe; lifting high the world's only Saviour, and doing so in such a way that his holy, all-embracing transforming love is reflected and authenticated in the dynamic diversity of their life together . . . I have a dream.

# Notes

## Preface

1. Not, perhaps, unlike Paul, who, in 1 Cor. 1:2, refers to 'all those everywhere who call on the name of our Lord Jesus Christ'.
2. According to some dictionary meanings, ethnicity and race are virtual equivalents. In general usage a distinction can be noted in that 'race' is commonly used with reference to the major divisions of humankind based on certain physical characteristics, notably colour difference, e.g. Caucasian (white), Negroid (black), Asiatic (yellow, brown). 'Ethnicity' is often used to refer to differentiations related to nationality, and hence to membership of a particular nation state, e.g. Chinese, French, Nigerian, Mexican. The usage adopted in this book will reflect that distinction.

## 1. What's this 'new-humanity' thing?

1. See Patrick Johnstone and Jason Mandryk, *Operation World*, Twenty-First Century Edition (Paternoster, 2001), p. 114.
2. Peter O'Brien, *The Letter to the Ephesians* (Apollos and Eerdmans, 1999), in an extended discussion of the central message of the letter, asserts: 'Ephesians 1:9–10 provides the key for unlocking the glorious riches of the letter' (p. 58).
3. James Denney, *Studies in Theology* (Hodder and Stoughton, 1904), p. 49.
4. William Hendriksen, *Exposition of Ephesians* (Baker, 1967), p. 129.
5. Tacitus, *History* 5.5.
6. William Barclay, *The Letters to the Galatians and the Ephesians* (St Andrew Press, 1958), p. 195.
7. From the hymn 'O come and mourn with me a while' by F. W. Faber.
8. So, for example, Peter O'Brien, who cites a recent study showing that when, in Paul, an aorist participle (here 'having slain'), follows the main verb (here 'might reconcile'), 'there is a definite tendency towards co-incidental action'. *The Letter to the Ephesians*, p. 205.

9. John Murray, cited in J. Douglas McMillan, *The Lord our Shepherd* (Evangelical Press of Wales, 1983), p. 14.

10. Harold H. Hoehner, *Ephesians: An Exegetical Commentary* (Baker, 2002), pp. 378–379. Cf. Stephen A. Rhodes, *The Challenge of Diversity: The Witness of Paul and the Gospels* (Fortress, 1996), p. 2.

11. This is clearly indicated by his use of the Greek verb *ktizō* here (verse 15): 'His purpose was to *create* one new humanity' (my italics), translating the Hebrew *bara*, which typically referred to God's creative acts, especially the bringing forth of that which did not previously exist (Gen. 1:1, 21, 27; Isa. 42:5; 45:8; Jer. 31:22; cf. Heb. 11:3).

12. 'The two elements . . . have become totally transformed in the process. This is the "third race" that is different from both Jews and Gentiles.' Andrew T. Lincoln, *Ephesians* (Word, 1990), pp. 143–144.

13. The background here is Isa. 52:7 and 57:19.

14. Lincoln, *Ephesians*, p. 162; cf. 2 Cor. 5:17: 'Anyone who belongs to Christ is a new person. The past is forgotten, and everything is new' (Contemporary English Version).

15. John A. Mackay, *God's Order: The Ephesians Letter and the Present Time* (Nisbet and Macmillan, 1953), p. 84.

16. F. F. Bruce, *The Epistle to the Ephesians* (Pickering and Inglis, 1961), pp. 321–322, 262.

17. Andrew Walls, *The Cross-Cultural Process in Christian History* (Orbis, 2002), pp. 72–78.

## 2. It's more than race

1. Johannes Blauw, *The Missionary Nature of the Church* (Lutterworth, 1974), p. 71.

2. The title was earned. 'The Galilee in which Jesus grew up included Assyrians, Babylonians, Egyptians, Macedonians, Persians, Romans, Syrians, and indigenous Canaanites . . . Jesus was raised in Galilee and influenced by this milieu.' Curtiss Paul DeYoung, Michael O. Emerson, George Yancey and Karen Chai Kim, *United by Faith: The Multicultural Congregation as an Answer to the Problem of Race* (Oxford University Press, 2003), p. 15.

3. David J. Bosch, *Witness to the World* (Marshall, Morgan and Scott, 1980), pp. 55–57. Cf. Matt. 11:5–6; Luke 4:16–30; cf. also Joachim Jeremias, *Jesus' Promise to the Nations* (SCM, 1959).

4. Bosch, *Witness to the World*, p. 19. Cf. also Johannes Verkuyl, who pictures Jesus 'itching with a holy impatience for that day when all the stops will be pulled as the message goes out to the Gentiles'; *Contemporary Missiology: An Introduction* (Eerdmans, 1978), p. 104; cited in Bosch, *Witness to the World*, p. 57.

5. John, reflecting, not for the only time, an independent, complementary tradition, refers to a Temple cleansing also at the outset of his ministry. Cf. Bruce Milne, *The Message of John*, The Bible Speaks Today (IVP, 1993), pp. 67–68.

6. See DeYoung *et al.*, *United by Faith*, p. 20.

7. Joachim Jeremias, *New Testament Theology* 1 (SCM, 1971), p. 109.

8. *Ibid.*, pp. 110–111.

9. *Ibid.*, p. 115.

10. Albert Nolan, *Jesus Before Christianity* (Orbis, 1978), p. 39.

11. Josephus, *Against Apion* 2.201.

12. Jeremias, *op. cit.*, p. 226.

13. Martin Luther, *A Commentary on St Paul's Epistle to the Galatians* (James Clarke, 1953), p. 272. Cf. Richard N. Longenecker, *Galatians*, Word Biblical Commentary (Word, 1990), p. 22, who speaks here of 'an exchange curse'.

14. Timothy George, *Galatians*, New American Commentary (Broadman and Holman, 1994), p. 284.

15. E. A. Judge, art. 'Roman Empire', *Illustrated Bible Dictionary* 3 (IVP, 1980), p. 1464.

16. See G. R. Beasley-Murray, *Baptism in the New Testament* (Macmillan, 1962), pp. 334–344.

17. Longenecker, *Galatians*, p. 69.

18. P. T. O'Brien, *Colossians, Philemon*, Word Biblical Commentary (Word, 1982), p. 192.

19. Tom Wright, *Paul for Everyone: Galatians and Thessalonians* (SPCK, 2002), p. 140.

20. M. J. Harris's rendering of 'Christ is all' (verse 12), in his *Colossians and Philemon* (Eerdmans, 1992), p. 155.

21. N. T. Wright, *Colossians and Philemon*, Tyndale New Testament Commentary (IVP, 1986), p. 140. Cf. also H. M. Carson, *The Epistles of Paul to the Colossians and Philemon*, Tyndale New Testament Commentary (Tyndale, 1960), p. 86: 'To say that Christ *is* all, is to assert that He so dominates the whole order of being that persons and

things have significance, not so much in their relation to each other, as in their relation to Him.'

22. On insights into achieving a unity in Christ that allows for diversities of Holy Spirit gifts, see J. I. Packer, *Keep in Step with the Spirit* (Fleming H. Revell, 1984), chapters 5 – 7; David Watson, *I Believe in the Church* (Hodder and Stoughton, 1978), pp. 341ff.; Donald Bridge and David Phypers, *Spiritual Gifts and the Church* (IVP, 1973), pp. 153ff.

23. Terry Griffiths, *Keep Yourselves from Idols: A New Look at 1 John* (Sheffield Academic Press, 2002). The view supported above is noted by Hans Windisch, *Die Katholischen Briefe* (Mohr, 1951), p. 115; cf. also discussion of the various possibilities here in I. H. Marshall, *The Epistles of John* (Eerdmans, 1978), pp. 134–138.

24. Andrew Walls, *The Cross-Cultural Process in Christian History* (Orbis, 2002), p. 75.

25. From the *Te Deum laudamus* in the *Book of Common Prayer*.

26. F. F. Bruce, *The Book of the Acts* (Marshall, Morgan and Scott, 1954), p. 64. Cf. David Lyon, 'Jesus in Disneyland: The Church meets the Postmodern Challenge', *ARC* (1994), p. 32: 'The social implications of Pentecost have yet to be elaborated for postmodern times, but this "anti-Babel" denies permanence to "Babel", and offers a profound perspective, a signpost in the mist, that reorientates those who mistook Babel for the terminus.'

27. Paul Pearce, 'Characteristics of Emerging Healthy Multicultural Churches', D.Min. thesis, McMaster University (April 2000), p. 16.

28. René Padilla, *op. cit.*, p. 151.

29. Michael Green, *Evangelism in the Early Church* (Hodder, 1970), p. 114.

30. Padilla, *op. cit.*, p. 152.

31. Ray Bakke, *A Theology as Big as the City* (IVP, 1997), pp. 145–146.

32. S. S. Bartchy, 'First-Century Slavery and the Interpretation of 1 Corinthians 7:21', Society of Biblical Literature Dissertation Series 11 (SBL, 1973), p. 137. Cf. also Gordon Fee, *The First Epistle to the Corinthians* (Eerdmans, 1987), p. 311: 'Paul's point is that God's gift . . . totally eliminates social setting as having any kind of religious significance.'

33. Edward Norman, cited in Alan Walker, *Christ is Enough* (Epworth, 1963), preface.

34. John R. W. Stott, *Romans: God's Good News for the World* (IVP, 1994), p. 395.

35. C. E. B. Cranfield, *The Epistle to the Romans* 2, International Critical Commentary (T. and T. Clark, 1979), p. 793; also J. B. Lightfoot, *St Paul's Epistle to the Romans* (Macmillan, 1868), p. 177, who refers to 'a fair presumption that among the salutations of the Epistle to the Romans some members at least of the imperial household are included'.

36. Stott, *Romans: God's Good News for the World*, p. 396.

37. So, for example, Paul Minear, *The Obedience of Faith* (SCM, 1971), pp. 16–17: 'The goal of *Romans* is, "Jews praising God among Gentiles, and Gentiles praising God along with his people" '.

38. Stott, *Romans: God's Good News for the World*, p. 397.

39. Pliny, *Epistles* 10.96–97, cited in F. F. Bruce, *The Spreading Flame* (Paternoster, 1958), pp. 170–171.

40. Aristides, cited in Martin Hengel, *Poverty and Riches in the Early Church* (Fortress, 1974), pp. 42–43.

41. *The First Apology of Justin the Martyr*, in Cyril C. Richardson (ed.), *Early Christian Fathers* (Macmillan, 1970), pp. 249–250.

42. Tertullian, *Apology* 39, trans. T. R. Glover (William Heinemann, 1931).

43. David Smith, 'The Church Growth Principles of Donald McGavran', *Transformation* (April–June 1985), p. 26.

44. Padilla, *op. cit.*, p. 165.

45. Green, *Evangelism in the Early Church*, pp. 117–118.

## 3. Underpinnings: doctrinal confirmations

1. Not a wholly imaginary being, but closely resembling someone who read a draft of the last chapter.

2. John Calvin, *Institutes* I.xiii.1, Library of Christian Classics 20 (SCM, 1961).

3. Augustine, *De Trinitate* 5.9. See Bruce Milne, *Know the Truth*, 2nd edn (IVP, 1998), pp. 75–80.

4. Stanley J. Grenz, *Revisioning Evangelical Theology* (IVP, 1993), p. 188.

5. In addition to the work of Grenz noted above, see Colin Gunton, *The One, the Three and the Many* (Cambridge University Press, 1993); and Miroslav Volf, *After Our Likeness: The Church as the Image of the Trinity* (Eerdmans, 1998).

6. David Clines, 'The Image of God in Man', *Tyndale Bulletin* 19 (1968), p. 100.

7. Cf. Karl Barth, 'The Doctrine of Creation', *Church Dogmatics* III/1 (T. and T. Clark, 1958), p. 116: 'The Fathers were right when they saw glimpses of the Trinity ... in Genesis 1.'

8. Stanley J. Grenz, *The Social God and the Relational Self* (Westminster/ John Knox, 2001), p. 332.

9. Parker J. Palmer, *The Courage to Teach* (Jossey-Bass, 1998), p. 9.

10. Ian Barbour, *Religion in an Age of Science* (Harper, 1990), p. 107 and *passim*.

11. Henry Stapp, quoted in Gary Zukav, *The Dancing Wu Li Masters* (Morrow, 1979), p. 94.

12. Luci Shaw, from 'Mary's Song', in *Accompanied by Angels: Poems of the Incarnation* (Eerdmans, 2006). Reproduced by permission.

13. C. S. Lewis, *Miracles* (Collins, 1947), title of chapter 14.

14. James Denney, *The Death of Christ* (Hodder and Stoughton, 1902), pp. 235–236.

15. Paul Pearce, 'It's Multi-Cultural Ministry for a Multi-Cultural World', *The Bridge* (April 1994).

16. Rudolf Schnackenburg, *The Church in the New Testament* (Burns and Oates, 1965), p. 165.

17. Emil Mersch, cited in J. A. T. Robinson, *The Body* (SCM, 1952), p. 58.

18. T. M. Lindsay, *The Church and the Ministry in the Early Centuries* (Hodder and Stoughton, 1902), p. 10.

19. Darrell L. Guder (ed.), *The Missional Church* (Eerdmans, 1998), pp. 232–233; citation from John Howard Yoder, *Royal Priesthood* (Eerdmans, 1994), pp. 113ff. Cf. also Gunton, *The One, the Three and the Many*, p. 217 n. 6: 'the local church is the first place where community is to be sought and found'; also Volf, *After Our Likeness*, p. 127, who cites with approval Webber's definition of the church as 'a visible assembly of visible persons at a specific place for specific action'.

20. G. R. Beasley-Murray, *Revelation*, New Century Bible (Eerdmans, 1974), p. 322; cf. also Bruce Milne, *The Message of Heaven and Hell*, The Bible Speaks today (IVP, 2002), pp. 318–319.

### 4. An idea whose hour has come: into the world of today

1. Andrew Walls, *The Cross-Cultural Process in Christian History* (T. and T. Clark, 2002), p. 76.

2. *Ibid.*, p. 78.

3. Alvin Toffler, *Future Shock* (Pan, 1970), p. 275.

4. Alvin Toffler, *The Third Wave* (Bantam, 1980), pp. 360–361.

5. Ray Bakke, *The Urban Christian* (IVP, 1987), p. 28. By 2050, out of a world population of some 9 billion, 7 billion are projected to be urban dwellers.

6. 'The Nation's Families, 1960–90', issued by the Joint Center for Urban Studies of MIT and Harvard.

7. Cited in Howard A. Snyder, *Earth Currents* (Abingdon, 1995), p. 11.

8. *Ibid.*, pp. 24–25.

9. David Held, *Global Transformations: Politics, Economics and Culture* (Oxford, 1999), p. 2.

10. Snyder, *Earth Currents*, p. 24. Not all observers are persuaded of the arrival of a radically new world at this point. See Richard Gibb, *Grace and Global Justice* (Paternoster, 2006), p. 211: 'However unevenly globalization is experienced throughout the world, the forces associated with this phenomenon are serving to transform state powers and the context in which they operate.'

11. Anthony Giddens, *Runaway World: How Globalization is Reshaping our Lives* (Profile, 1999), p. 7.

12. Roland Robertson, *Global Modernities* (Sage, 1995), pp. 25–44.

13. Peter Dray, *Globalization and the Christian Mission*, Global Connections Occasional Paper 15 (Autumn 2003) (Evangelical Missionary Alliance), p. 2.

14. James S. Stewart, *A Faith to Proclaim* (Hodder and Stoughton, 1953), pp. 115–116.

15. David Aikman, *Jesus in Beijing* (Regnery Publishing, 2003; Monarch Books, 2005), p. 49.

## 5. It's happened before: the first-century world

1. E. A. Judge, art. 'Roman Empire', *Illustrated Bible Dictionary* 3 (IVP, 1980), p. 1344.

2. Bruce Metzger, *The New Testament: Its Background, Growth and Content* (Abingdon, 1965), p. 30. There is interesting evidence of this 'Roman model' within the New Testament. When Jesus was brought to trial he was in effect faced with a double judicial examination, first before the Jewish Sanhedrin (Mark 14:53–65), and then secondly before the Roman imperial authority in the person of Pilate (Mark 15:1–15).

3. F. F. Bruce, *Commentary on the Epistle to the Colossians* (Marshall, Morgan and Scott, 1957), p. 277.

4. Kenneth Scott Latourette, *A History of Christianity* (Harper, 1953), p. 84.

5. John Poulton, *People Under Pressure* (Lutterworth, 1973), p. 112, (my italics).

6. Alvin Toffler, *The Third Wave* (Bantam, 1980), p. 374.

7. Alvin Toffler, *Future Shock* (Pan, 1970), p. 293.

8. Karl Marx, 'On the Jewish Question', *Karl Marx, Frederick Engels: Collected Works 3* (Lawrence and Wishart, 1975), pp. 167–168.

9. U. Duchrow, cited in Klaus Bochmuehl, *The Challenge of Marxism* (IVP, 1980), p. 48. The use Paul's phrase from Eph. 2:15 is striking. Cf. Vladimir Illyich Lenin, *What Is To Be Done?* (Progress Publishers, 1967).

10. Walter Lippmann, cited in George Sweeting, *Great Quotes and Illustrations* (Word, 1985), p. 187.

### 6. Widening the view: other dimensions of community

1. Parker J. Palmer, *The Courage to Teach* (Jossey-Bass, 1998), pp. 89–90 (my italics).

2. Robert Louis Stephenson, *Dr Jekyll and Mr. Hyde* (The Folio Society, 1948), pp. 19–20.

3. Blaise Pascal, quoted in Stuart Barton Babbage, *The Mark of Cain* (Paternoster, 1966), p. 35.

4. Henri Nouwen, *Walk with Jesus: Stations of the Cross* (Orbis, 1990), p. 35; cf. also M. Scott Peck, *The Different Drum: Community Making and Peace* (Touchstone, 1987), pp. 53–56.

5. Regrettably, the number is growing rather than receding at the present time: *Operation World*, twenty-first-century edition (Paternoster, 2001), p. 15, for example, cites in only one country – Chile – between 1,000 and 5,000 denominations, 'with one or two starting every week'.

6. James I. Packer and Thomas C. Oden (eds.), *One Faith: The Evangelical Consensus* (IVP, 2004).

7. Cf. Timothy George and John Woodbridge, *The Mark of Jesus* (Moody, 2005), who champion the quest for evangelical unity on the basis of a series of simple principles.

### 7. Down to earth: the new-humanity church: its worship and leadership

1. Michael O. Emerson and Christian Smith, *Divided by Faith* (Oxford, 2000), p. 135.

2. It is instructive to read 1 Cor. 12:15–17, substituting 'seniors' for 'foot', and 'young people' for 'hand'; or 'Caucasian whites' for 'ear', and 'ethnically different' for 'eye', etc. The familiar passage suddenly takes on remarkable new dimensions of meaning, a meaning that in my judgment is exactly what Paul is actually saying here. In other words, we perhaps begin to 'hear' it for the first time.

3. J. B. Torrance, *Worship, Community and the Triune Grace of God* (IVP, 1996), p. 14.

4. See the work of Robert E. Webber, including *Worship Old and New* (Zondervan, 1994); and *Blended Worship* (Hendrikson, 1996).

5. Darrell L. Guder (ed.), *The Missional Church* (Eerdmans, 1998), pp. 229.

6. Michael Moynagh, *Changing World, Changing Church* (Monarch, 2001), p. 143.

7. Jess Moody, cited in Sweeting, *Great Quotes and Illustrations*, p. 175.

8. Richard Baxter, *The Reformed Pastor* (SCM, 1956), pp. 50, 75.

9. Cf. for example the standards for elders and deacons in the pastoral letters: 1 Tim. 3:1–7; Titus 1:7–9.

10. Sheila Cassidy, *Sharing the Darkness* (Orbis, 1991), p. 35.

## 8. Down to earth: discipleship and fellowship in the new-humanity church

1. See Stanley J. Grenz, *Welcoming but not Affirming: An Evangelical Response to Homosexuality* (Westminster, 1998); Thomas Schmidt, *Straight and Narrow?* (IVP, 1995); Robert A. J. Gagnon, *The Bible and Homosexual Practice: Texts and Hermeneutics* (Abingdon, 2001).

2. Thomas Long, *The Witness of Preaching* (Westminster/John Knox, 1989), p. 80.

3. See Walter Ong, *The Presence of the Word: Some Prolegomena for Cultural and Religious History* (Yale University Press, 1967); Q. J. Schultze, *The Habits of the High-Tech Heart* (Baker, 2002); Neil Postman, *Technopoly: The Surrender of Culture to Technology* (Vintage, 1992).

4. 'The human impossibility of the Church's proclamation consists simply in the impossibility of the attempt to speak for God . . . Saying that what happens here is human frailty is far too weak an expression. It is not frailty, it is death. This is not difficulty, it is sheer impossibility.' Karl Barth, *Church Dogmatics* I/2 (T. and T. Clark, 1956), p. 750.

5. Paul Tournier, *A Place for You* (SCM, 1968), p. 170.

6. Howard A. Snyder, *The Community of the King* (IVP, 1977), p. 143.
7. C. S. Lewis, *Mere Christianity* (Harper, 1952), p. 205.
8. See Bruce Milne, *We Belong Together* (IVP, 1978).
9. C. H. Spurgeon, *An All-Round Ministry* (Banner of Truth, 1960), p. 47.
10. Jerry Cook, *Love, Acceptance and Forgiveness* (Regal Books, 1979), pp. 12–13.
11. Gerd Theissen, *Sociology of Early Palestinian Christianity* (Fortress, 1978), pp. 111–112.
12. Martin Luther King Jr, *Strength to Love* (Hodder, 1973), p. 36.
13. Billy Graham, typescript of *Message to Christian Workers* (Nairobi, 1959).
14. From her hymn 'Father, I know that all my life'.
15. John Calvin, *The Institutes of the Christian Religion* 1 (SCM, 1961), I.iii.5.

## 9. A heart for the world: mission and evangelism in the new-humanity church

1. Larry L. McSwain, 'A Critical Appraisal of the Church Growth Movement', *Review and Expositor* 77/4 (Fall 1980), p. 530.
2. Cited in Donald W. McCullough, *The Trivialization of God* (Navpress, 1995), p. 40.
3. René Padilla, *Let the Earth Hear His Voice* (Worldwide, 1975), p. 131. See also David J. Bosch, *Transforming Mission: Paradigm Shifts in Theology of Mission* (Orbis, 1991), p. 81.
4. C. Peter Wagner, *Our Kind of People: The Ethical Dimensions of Church Growth in America* (John Knox, 1979), p. 147.
5. Michael O. Emerson and Christian Smith, *Divided by Faith* (Oxford, 2000).
6. For the United States the population figures are startling. Numbers of people of colour have more than doubled in the USA between 1960 and the present. In absolute numbers, the USA had well over 35 million *more* people of (beautiful?) colour in 2000 than it did in 1980 – more people than lived in the entire USA during the Civil War period of the 1860s.
7. Curtiss Paul DeYoung, Michael O. Emerson (one of the co-authors of *Divided by Faith*), George Yancey and Karen Chai Kim, *United by Faith: The Multicultural Congregation as an Answer to the Problem of Race* (Oxford University Press, 2003). The authors define 'multi-racial' as having no single ethnic group as more than 80% of the whole (which currently describes no more than 7.5% of America's 300,000 congregations).

8. 'All Churches Should be Multiracial', *Christianity Today* (April 2005), p. 35. The article features the testimony of Bill Hybels, founder and senior minister of Willowcreek Community Church in South Barrington, Illinois. He writes (p. 38): 'Willow Creek started in the era when the church growth people were saying, "Don't dissipate your energies fighting race issues. Focus everything on evangelism." It was the homogeneous unit principle of church growth. And I remember thinking: *That's true*. I didn't know whether I wanted to chance alienating people who were seekers, whose eternity was on the line, and who might only come to church one time ... So now, 30 years later, as I read *Divided by Faith* I recognize that a true biblically functioning community must include being multiracial. My heart beats so fast for that vision today. I marvel at how naïve and pragmatic I was 30 years ago.'

9. Luci Shaw, *God in the Dark* (Regent College Publications, 1989), pp. 127–128.

10. Reynolds Price, cited in Philip Yancey, *The Jesus I Never Knew* (Zondervan, 1995), p. 269.

11. Quoted in Desmond Doig, *Mother Teresa: Her People and Her Work* (Collins, 1976), p. 159.

12. Ray Bakke, *The Urban Christian* (IVP, 1987), p. 43.

13. *Ibid.*, p. 57.

14. Samuel Escobar, *Global Missiology for the 21st Century* (Baker, 2000), p. 26.

## 10. Riding the wave: the challenges and opportunities of new-humanity churches in today's and tomorrow's worlds

1. Tertullian could challenge Rome's pagan rulers in his *Apology* of 197 AD: 'We are but of yesterday, and yet we have filled all the places that belonged to you – cities, islands, forts, towns, exchanges, the military camps, tribes, town councils, the palace, the senate, the market-place, we have left you nothing but your temples.' Tertullian, *Apology*, 37:4.

2. Howard A. Snyder, *Earth Currents*, p. 24.

3. Justo L. Gonzalez, *For the Healing of the Nations: The Book of Revelation in an Age of Cultural Conflict* (Maryknoll, 1999), p. 91.

4. Stanley J. Grenz, *A Primer on Postmodernism* (Eerdmans, 1996), p. 44.

5. C. Jeff Woods, *Congregational Megatrends* (Alban Institute, 1996), p. 10.

6. A phrase we coined in Vancouver to help focus our response to the diversity we were encountering all around us in the course of our ministry.

7. John Poulton, *People Under Pressure* (Lutterworth, 1973), p. 112.

8. Ronald Sider, *The Scandal of the Evangelical Conscience* (Baker, 2005).

9. What follows is based, of course, on the speech delivered by Martin Luther King Jr on the steps of the Lincoln Memorial on 28 August 1963.

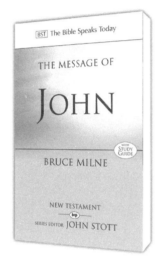